TIM

ANNE CLUYSENAAR

TIMESLIPS

New and Selected Poems

CARCANET

First published in 1997 by
Carcanet Press Limited
4th Floor, Conavon Court
12-16 Blackfriars Street
Manchester M3 5BQ

A CIP catalogue record for this book
is available from the British Library
ISBN 1 85754 267 3

The publisher acknowledges financial assistance
from the Arts Council of England

Set in 10pt Palatino by Bryan Williamson, Frome
Printed and bound in England by SRP Ltd, Exeter

Acknowledgements

Acknowledgements are due to the editors of the following anthologies and magazines.

Anthologies: *Aquarius Women; Book in a Day; Hepworth, A Celebration; Lancaster Arts Festival Poems; New Poets of Ireland; Pequod; 27 British Poets; Poetry Introduction 4; The Virago Book of Love Poetry; Westwords.*

Magazines: *Continuum; The Dubliner; The Dublin Magazine; The Irish Times; Phoenix; Poetry Wales; New Welsh Review; Planet; 'Red Poets' Society; Resurgence; Sheaf; The So What? Factory; Swansea Review.*

Some of the poems have also been broadcast on *Poetry Now* (BBC Radio 3) and on Radio Telefis Eireann.

The poems grouped here as 'On the Skyline', 'Poems of Memory' and 'Open Ways' are from *Double Helix* (1982).

For Walt

Contents

Poems from *Nodes*
  Shadow   12
  Flight   14
  Petrarch   16
  Figures   18
  Epithalamium   20
  The Fawn   22
  Sea   24

Metamorphoses 1965
  Orpheus   29
  Europa   29
  Actaeon   30
  Ariadne   30
  Hellespont   31

Occasional Poems 1966-68
  La Belle Otero   35
  Owl   35
  Too Much More   36
  Life's Edges   36
  An Intermittent Thought   37
  Exhaustion   37
  Presences   38
  Death   38
  Maker   39

On the Skyline
  A Dangerous Road   43
  In Time Lapse   45
  He Took His Father's Advice   47
  Letters and Memoirs   48
  The Line on the Map   50
  On the Skyline   52
  Resting the Ladder   54
  Beyond Reason   55

Poems of Memory   59

Open Ways
  Open Ways   69
  Braille   70
  Ready to Leave   71
  On the Turn   72
  Divided   73
  Signs   74
  Memories   75
  About the Church   76
  Double Light   77

Poems based on Visual Materials
  Cauldron Rituals   81
  Cycladic Head Haiku   84
  Clay   85
  River Form   86

Timeslips
  Landfall   89
  In a Gap of Light   92
  Nudging the Margins   95
  Dark Mothers   97
  Solstice   99
  Quarry   102
  Winged as They Are   104
  Borders   105
  Drawing Breath   107
  Timeslips   108
  Natural History   110

Words for Music
  If Mind Remember   115
  A Trace Known   117
  Esther   120

Vaughan Variations   127

Coda
Magnolia   165
Stag Beetle   166
Butterflies   168
Smoke   169
Guilt   170
Yellow Meadow-Ants in Hallowed Ground   172
Cave Trout   173
A Matter of Scale   175

Poems from

NODES

Shadow

Reflections break into the shadow, like
the wings of a white butterfly or thought
visible in the pulse of a closed eyelid.

Foliage echoes in its arches the blunt
explosions of light behind it, in brightening
sequence, silhouetted, translucent, shining,

descending to a sea which suspends the beat
of fear, like the first sun after snowfall
or the first touch between potential lovers.

That warm second of safety, a bird
on the wing, drops singing out of sight,
in its beak the olive-branch of my peace,

but sings again in a remembered place,
a round oleander enamelled with flowers
between narrow-windowed walls, at the foot

of a long flight of stone steps
leading out of sunlight and into a church
whose vaults are dazzled by a golden altar.

My fancy wanders there with frail pleasure,
fearing to see, in those familiar beauties
of holy family and hovering dove

inhuman visions, which even he, perhaps,
who placed with perfect passion the bright
arches and hanging fruits of his orchards

to frame the morning of his wife and child,
hated. For sins of insufficient love.
And for the repeated disappointment of art.

Whatever knowledge of light and shade
this was, that stopped short of prophecy
but, by a fear whose action is protective,

circled her brow with a filament of gold,
it consecrates the morning, then as now,
holding doubt breathless at that point

past which one cannot go without faith,
or duplicity, or pride, or long tradition,
or the authority of a trained imagination.

Flight

In memory of Percy Lubbock

Graceful, with ungainly cries
of appeasement, with sharp wings
cupped at the fountains of the air,

swallow, for whatever eyes
recall you, with their wings
of sight folded, hear this prayer.

And hear it for those eyes' sake
that copy from your tumbling wings,
sweetness, a charm against the dark.

Though floods should overtake
eyesight or will, may those wings
bring joy to the soul's ark.

And if on your lilting flight
the bells of Sunday and the sea
with all its almond breakers

blossoming, adorably modulate,
so may my love, over the sea
of time and its great breakers.

soar and sing, always
by every atom that in the sea
holds and is held, accompanied.

And may other lovers, on days
like this, when the dark sea
is appeased, have their love accepted.

But O how lost the swallow
tumbling in the white light
of morning, how like its own

invisible and voiceless shadow
hovering between layers of light!
Between sight and thought, my own

shadow, my soul's sorrow,
hovers invisible in delight.
And that this joy be love's own

for life, may my soul borrow
grace of the swallow's flight,
blessing and blessed in its own.

Petrarch

Is it true that you never, of all
your women, handled your elected lover
though her beauty yielded itself to a verbal

courting? Surely you took your images for her
from twenty years' more confident lovemaking,
those faultless images of physical splendour?

Were you afraid of her fine body changing,
of your patience with human love, untried
by her, but which failed with others, failing?

And was it for charity or love or pride
that you set to work with rhymes and reasons
to justify her chastity, caution or pride?

When from your window you saw the seasons
changing, but always fulfilled, did you repent,
for love of this one woman, of whatever reasons

could not support more compassionate argument,
your quill left dry before the poem's close,
your room, save only river-song, left silent?

Perhaps after all it was so, who knows?
At the still pool, whose overflow is the river,
lost in a blond shadow of beech-groves,

these two, so tortuous when not together,
lie stilled, numb with the drink of love,
Petrarch without speech, without pride Laura.

So it may have been. And a white glove,
flung down in haste among the flowers, later,
in laughing haste, searched for, for fear of . . .

It may have been so. Not a fortunate passion.
Coincidence of time and place so rare
for them, and the years so prompt with poison.

But he, from his window, might see her hair
in the sun-plaits of the shallow river and,
in the slow twist of a trout from black to silver,

see the languid twist of her white hand
out of the garment's fold – so laying bare
his heart, in this, for her to understand.

Figures

A slim wave's shadow
sinks into the hammered gold
of dry stone creased with water.

Fish become concentrations
of light, on which waves wind
tongue-rolls of clear water.

Woven by ripples from beneath
into a veil of blown silk,
reflections hesitate on the water.

Intense figures of happiness,
traced as by a falling star
on black mind or on water.

Fish over sharp shadows,
opaque in blurred sunlight,
relax in the swift water.

Day between dawn and dark.
Hills pale and rough with summer.
Rippling stillness of open water.

Silence possesses the spirit,
a kiss without a message
at love's point of balance.

Through almost unmoving water
pulses race to the shore
where the lake loses its balance.

A silk scarf, rippling
rapidly at eye level,
throws the fields off balance.

But hills flow up unmoving
from swifter waves of grass
to make the horizon balance.

The variant self awakes
to hills, fields, open water,
newly aware of their stillness.

Between a kiss and the stillness
of lonely thought, water
off balance on a lonely shore.

Epithalamium

The rings of the sun rise
in cloud above them. A quiver
of wind on the pane becomes

the quiver in his arms of her
sleeping flanks. And through these
echoes extends love's power.

Wings open and shut, the sun
thick in their fans, they flash
on his thought her body's turn.

Dawn has melted their flesh
to a fan of shadows, thrown
the spread fan beyond reach

now, in their double darkness,
shutting. Sleep, then, sleep.
The rings of the sun's expanse

rest in her body. Timeless,
your love. It circles a deep
night, without fear of darkness.

Traced in the rise and fall
of wings, day at your window
eddies without noise. Able

to hold her body now so
still, remember the ceremonial
opaque berries of mistletoe

shining from within flights of
dark leaves, as you shine
from within the shadows of

her limbs, the year's crown.
Such loving moments have
within dark ones grown.

Not without wisdom the tide
of day is met with praise
or time wasted with pride

if, without fear, without tears,
you should see again, at her side,
the rings of a winter sunrise.

The Fawn

With the grace of a great hind,
the fawn Love at her side,
summer hangs back in the mind.

I see her eyes grow wide
watching the leaves unwind,
the water clear, the spotted

forest ruffle in the sun
its masses of winter dark,
restless as the red fawn

that stirs uncertainly, look,
stretches and sleeps again,
its dream caught up in the wake

of the wind. The fawn is dreaming
peace, and the golden gloom
of the forest has it in keeping.

But summer hangs back, for whom
the hound and bugle sing
beyond spring's golden gloom.

Winter will come and then,
under the leaves' blue fall,
whiter than skin and bone

the snow will cover all.
No trace of hind or fawn
but, where the waterfall

breaks on the rock, a great
skeleton sprawls, that knew
the hunting tooth of fate

and sunlight and the blue
branch of a drink so sweet
it flowered as flowers do,

cool in the golden body,
before the hounds were heard,
the chase begun and, weary,

the leap to silence made.
Black as the bowl of a tree
the grown stag lifts his head.

Sea

Your touches fade from my body
into the open sea of absence
where time gathers without pity.

There can be no future happiness,
you said, and your eyes were open
as the sea when storm threatens.

Love is not love, O love, which can
choose of the lover the present only.
Change is the tide of love's ocean.

Familiar as the rising sun,
our meeting renews whatever, earlier,
we shared of love's first dawn,

I, bewildered by the racing stars,
you, gazing from the winter mountain.
We met then, despite years and countries.

And if, in half-sleep, the fear
returns, of our shared memories,
think – they helped us to recognise each other.

Your touches fade from my body
into the open sea of absence
where time gathers without pity.

There can be no future loss,
my love, since our eyes are open
to the sea whose storm threatens.

Love, is not love, O love, which can
choose of the lover the present only.
Change is the tide of love's ocean.

And if only once the rising sun
were to rise, if only once more
we were to meet, my precious one,

I, watching the falling stars,
you, alone on the winter mountain,
we should be together in time's spaces.

And if, in half-sleep, the fear
returns, of our shared memories,
think – They helped us to love each other.

METAMORPHOSES

1965

1 Orpheus

In memory of my mother

As though it moved through rock
The mind of the poet searches
Down resisting thought for the dark
Centre which no song expresses.

There, unlit by time,
Our axle of change and growth
Revolves on a point of creation.
There, for us, is death.

Constantly flowing, like a poem
From the mind's vanishing-point,
An atom is born of each atom
To sustain time's light.

Though she is dead, she was,
And became herself through time.
Her memory lives in life-praise,
And at the point of creation.

2 Europa

Across an increasing silence
Of open ocean,
Through brighter and darker waves
Dealt from the horizon,

Astride the straining back,
Through winds colder
Than fear, Europa, take
His impersonal desire.

If Zeus once again
That journey made
From the shadowlessness of heaven
To incarnate shade,

Now on your shaking body
And spirit he depends.
Through them, through them only,
His divinity returns.

3   Actaeon

How from her fingers those rings
Of light, fondling the quiet surface,
Slide away, while her hair cascades
In gold over her warm shoulders.

Silence of her eyes at gaze,
Forgetful of the target's outlines,
Brooding on the blurred waters
Their silk-sliding at her thighs.

Lightly through shifting leaves
Rustle a thousand drops and beams
Penetrating the green flanges,
The white, of pool and leaves' reflections.

Silence, silence, my heart! Is
This moment the moment for her eyes
To be raised, to curse love, yours, hers?
For you to kneel to death in the chase?

4   Ariadne

His black sails tighten against the storm.
Now, my thread no longer guides him.
Aching, the ropes, the voices die away.
A million waves increase the sea's cry.

O Theseus, had your love guided,
I should have come to the last fold
Of the heart, and your suffering
Violence appeased with my own suffering.

But now Fate has cut all threads away.
On this island shore where only
Dionysus' most solitary ecstasies
Remain, meaningful suffering fails.

He draws with him the powerful winds
That carry his ship to the Kingdom of Athens.
The stars are bright again in the darkness.
O but my heart is an emptier stillness.

5 Hellespont

Like life itself, always and never given,
You who refuse love all reassurance
But the undeniable, the ever-unspoken,
Must give yourself as no man is given

Who can mask in himself life's intransigence.
For you, what stress between delight and pain
Governs the hurtled planet's balance
Through invisible, familiar, infinite space!

You reach me exhausted from the waves
But in your heart, the strength of that ocean
Which you overcame. You touch me with diffidence,
The reverence of the creator towards the creation.

On the night when at last you find no shore
I shall know directly for the first time
Those waves which you have tasted as you come
Silent, with salt lips, from such horror.

OCCASIONAL POEMS

1966-68

La Belle Otero

A mouth closed on the tips of the lips,
the brows tilted like cruising wings,
a look distant, helpless, proud,
the long animal nose, the fatally low
forehead, unequipped for thought's bleakness.

With what self-mutilating satisfaction
the papers publish, side by side,
the misty massive hair, the beringed fingers
and, sixty years later, the upturned collar,
the cotton scarf plumped to conceal the throat.

Not the changes, the narrowed shoulders, hidden hands,
facial flesh sagging as under a thumbprint
(illustrating, they say, that all passes),
not the changes, but the inhabited skull,
the strangely similar gaze in two chance moments –
these mutilate unforeseeably, like the look
of death on a loved face peacefully sleeping.
This gaze from, and into, an unexchangeable fate.

Owl

In my fingers, in their naked heat,
the tiny body shrinks its blood,
flicks the saucered eye-feathers.
Along the pale rims of the eyes
flecks of dry blood, like the intimate stippling
on the vagina of a wild flower.

Too Much More

Trying to do too much more than exist
soon all life is stopped at the source.
Under the eye of a researching soul,
a small creature, lacking the power of discourse,
submits at the end of its ever-decreasing circle
to a demonstrative, paws-in-air paralysis.

But is the soul then finally content?
Yes. It massages with the long finger of sloth
that almost inanimate, awaiting heart
until the automatic muscle draws breath
and a fine, almost forgotten art
of living, sets the animal again on its feet.

Life's Edges

The struggle of sleep
dissolves into day's peace.
Merest coincidences
remake life's edges.

Across the dawning carpet
a dew of sunlight.
Your body moves to come near,
cool and unconscious as water.

The empty darkness has faltered
again, and retreated.
How fresh now the wide sand,
the blurred glow of its grains.

An Intermittent Thought

The house shakes in the wind, like a ship.
The masses of outside matter break loose again.
Bricks crumble against the earth's weight.

Here there is safety, but not much,
while the heart persists, an intermittent thought,
a door banging and banging in the night.

Exhaustion

When the mind has lost its grasp
like a hand soft with exhaustion,

and the world slips and falls
despite the desperately contracted muscle,

in that moment the heart,
weak with unpractised love,
no, even now, should not be powerless.

Presences

That mute movement outside, this doubling
muteness of my closer body in which I,
seeking whatever it is that is,
am no more than my own words . . . What,
in this small space, is it that circles
invisibly, and holds in its prisoner's hands
a huge reality, invisible as the universe?
And is alone again in the pressure of presences?

Out of the foreknown but never to be known,
the being-dead, and the known aloneness of life,
by chance I have escaped,
unexpectedly heavy with gifts born of silence:
a white tablecloth of nothing, with magical
food and wine, a discovered road through darkness
leading safely to undiscoverable ends.

Death

Eventually the sequence of living
becomes the structure of life. Death,
for all it matters, might have been the beginning.
Before birth, too, our absence is endless.

Maker

Her pen-tip drives its brief rivers
into the destroyed forest, snow-white
under her thinking fingers.
She foretells from disorders of private thought
wars of the world-spirit,
a fisherman's hand covered with ash.
As she writes, the present falters,
always fugitive, in the slow light:
her own past face in the mirror
like the light of the farthest star,
her thoughts dead when they reach paper.
All the same, when she leaves work,
the world is loosed about her senses,
with milk rushing over a polished brim,
bread falling brightly wide under the knife
and love awaiting her body's question.

ON THE SKYLINE

'To keep alive the wonder of suffering
You have been metamorphosed into me.'
– Anna Akhmatova, Summer 1915.

A Dangerous Road

A dangerous road: many people,
including friends of ours, have died
somewhere along these bends
above the heavenly valley
whose dips and rises, never mind
how well we walk them,
remain the mysterious features
of a dream, disposed by chance
in eternally changing beauty.
Corn, shadow, snow-patch, copse, wall.
Lemon and dark. Furred, smooth. Roads hidden.

Before we married, I used to pass
on my way south, your warnings
warm in my ear, but driving fast.
Now, I drive slowly to work,
taking more care for both our sakes.
This morning, as my favourite bend
brought Wortley into sight, close
round its church and the pub that
we drank at, testing for rumours
of a place like the one we found,
I hear myself speak: 'I wouldn't mind
if I got killed along here.'
An Irish thought, you'll say,
if not too shocked to joke me.
And it's fanciful, too,
if I meant my body would stay here.
Not sure what I had in mind,
I do know that behind the message
lies a way of life whose voice,
newly mine, was always the speech
of those who have somewhere to live.
Our local church handbook tells
how work on the Old Woodhead Tunnel
brought 'terrible accidents' and the dead
left, often, no more than a nickname,
an accent and an age for the vicar's records.

But those men, buried out of sight
round the valley's turn, had their own
chances, unknown to their loving ones.
Like this, unknown to you. Tonight,
making light of it, I know I'll turn
the memory to thankful praise
of your love, even more of yourself
and of all who, like you, can love.

Against the sun, on my way home,
I drive entranced by these white fields
dipping, rising to sombre hills.
Near the roadway, a few sheep
graze, swaddled in light,
and beeches mass to a veined amber.
Safe in the car, struck only by
a dangerous doubt, I hear the voice again
(it is a day for voices): 'But others
see this the same way', the beauty, the meaning of matter,
'and who do you want to speak to, but others?'

In Time-Lapse

In time-lapse, falling, rising,
our lives create, again and again,
for the world, moments of self-knowing.
Joy or sorrow, for all the difference matters,
tears the unique solitary fabric
from which consciousness flows beyond,
wave on wave, our million biographies
obliterated. Footprints at high tide.

As, without silence, speech is nothing,
so my love for you is nothing without this nothing.
You are what will never be again, a sentence
made out of the world to tell me love.
And love, even as it wavers, is enough
to hold sacred the meanings of life,
faults, failures, conditions, coincidences,
ludicrous courageous details to which we witness
through our only forever.
                              In the perfect republic,
Milosz says, 'they walk contemplating
the holy word: Is – so early in the morning
that the sun has barely made it through the dense maples.'
Here, the sun barely makes it at all, the rain
mildews, day after summer day, our bank of dog roses:
the roses of such true, wild, simple love
that poets dare no longer mention them!
All the same, some ignoramus who never heard
of poetry, is walking down here, so early,
by the stream, and stops to look, thinking himself alone,
while his black dog pursues something more interesting.

Thoughts that are part of my world, as are mine
of his, pass silently on with his hunched figure
into the drizzle: he crosses the bridge out of sight.
The moment can never be otherwise. Together
we rest in it, it is a footprint
fossilised on a shore, the silt
of words happening to drift this way
with the obliterating tide.

                              So matter, sometimes,
sees itself, as it rises and falls,
and leaves a record of what is anyway immortal.
'If not I, then someone else,' wrote Milosz,
'would be walking here, trying to understand . . .
I was not necessary.' The unnecessary poet,
the man with the dog, are ciphers, the conversation
of matter with itself. In which I is truly another.

And who needs to be necessary, except to those
whose love is witness? It is enough
to recognise, to be recognised, and the rest
is the price of love. A small price even.
I think this, and watch the impossible thought
like a wave, now white, now black,
travel away, beyond and over us.

He Took His Father's Advice

*'We . . . will always be glad to hear all your news but bear in
mind that a little written carefully and well will be of greater
advantage to yourself that volumes of careless and hurried
writing . . .'*
       – written to my grandfather by his father, Dublin, 1 August 1869.

He took his father's advice. Carefully and well
he censored the news of life, both to others
and to himself.
            His dress sword meets earth
at a determined angle, though the tip
dips into shadow. He chose his wives
for a sensitive weakness he made sure to lack.
Death and madness removed them, through childbirth,
child loss. It must have seemed that all acts
of creation were dangerous. He had no use
for women's nature-babble, the maintenance
of long-distance affection. And in fact their words
were unfit for disaster. They died or broke down
in silence, their tears like their deeper joys
private to the end, their intimate letters
burnt by a sensible household as signs of madness.
The decorous cry, art's double helix,
was not in their tradition.
            Refusing to have madness
home, in the shape of his wife, he wasted away
to die quiet, military language likewise
not to the purpose. Only that other helix,
of live tissue, continues their argument,
joining with other voices, linking and sharing
ancient opposing wisdoms to new purposes.
Which have changed little, though their contexts change.

In the photo, his balance is assured by one foot
and that useless sword. The other foot
hesitates, as in life, between stance and step.

Letters and Memoirs

Letters and memoirs seem to tell me less
than this luminous fossil – so strictly posed,
a band of metal just visible at the neck,
keeping the stance steady: this true image
of a bond neither could afterwards recall.
The details are enigmatic. I peer closely,
deciphering each hair, each youthful wrinkle
in grandmother's smile, the shining lower lip,
soft, surely loving, the large capable hand
on which my mother's fist, clenched in delight,
has left a tender shadow.
                  I read through letters
written to sister, mother, at home in England.
She had broken down already, just after marriage,
and soon (before mother was ten) she'd be taken away
to unvisited mental homes, whose names are forgotten.
The letters are those of a woman with few enjoyments,
all of them private, none trivial. A lawn robe
for baby. A view. A puppy. A cool morning garden.
A rare picnic with the husband she hardly mentions.

Scanning the print, left on that alien light
of another country, another century,
Muree, India, eighteen-ninety-four,
I recognise, in this way of holding her first-born –
temple to temple at shoulder height – the love
my mother gave me, forty-two years later.
Forty-two years later still, as I calculate
forward and backward in time, I seek the words
that will pose my feeling.
                  Photographed in rock,
the fragile shapes of our ancestors flow still
on the drift of a tide turned these three million years.
They settled just so, one day, one forgotten moment.
I lay the two prints together.
                  Christmas has passed.
Among our cards, no haloed Mother and Child
tempts us to sentiments we can't abide by.

Outside, as the year begins, snow falls like silt,
the worst since childhood for us in our middle age.

The typewriter drops its silt into the silence.
Those hours, and these, in all their details of writing,
of reading, are now invisible fossils that no one
could recall. All the prints are laid down together.

The Line on the Map

The line on the map has become hills, trees,
a place, not a direction. The lines of her memoir
merge into realities, a white house,
my life overlapping hers across seventy years.
I check all the details, and find everything
except the pollarded willow in whose giant cup,
running over with light, she escaped the world –
and found it, looking through the long shoots
into the distance. Rotted by too many rains,
the tree is gone and I have only myself
to hold, for an afternoon, to this overflow,
a spring light such as I know she loved.
There is a smell of early hay, black earth
breathes through the long grasses and has risen,
delicate, through wild rose and harebell.

Housman came here, in memory of a lad
who lived in this house before my mother did
and killed himself for loss of the vicar's daughter.
Cradley churchyard commemorates him and uncle,
sons of The Halesand who died too young,
though in different wars. Housman praised him,
knowing that a soul undone may undo others.
>   'Shot? So quick, so clean an ending?
>   Oh that was right, lad, that was brave:
>   Yours was not an ill for mending,
>   'Twas best to take it to the grave.'
Brave. But bravest? Best? More difficult,
anyway, the et ceteras of survival,
the surprise of love beyond love's end.

I talk with the daughter of the house. We stand
together under the copper beech and she shows me,
here, how a branch curves to a child-sized seat.
She used to be swung in it so that the sun dazzled
through the dark dome.

                              I remind myself
how far apart we might have seemed, she and I,
meeting elsewhere. And from under the day's brightness
slides that social shadow, which might have divided me
from grandmother, mother, uncle. Possession. Dispossession.
Love unoffered across so many frontiers, not least
those of politics in the name of humanity.

                                          We walk across
the perfect lawn to the tea-table, still set where I know,
from photographs, my mother's family gathered
on long summer evenings before the First World War.
There is nothing here to waken unkindness.
We talk of the record the garden and house afford
of owners come and gone over centuries,
additions, removals. When they tarmacked the yard
they kept back a patch of cobble: in this photo,
we see how my mother on her dapple-grey
poses on just that patch! I feel myself
afloat on circumstance, as they were, a living core
strangely unchanging from one life to another.
The past. Today. The future. Beyond love's end.

In the churchyard, the daisies lean to the light,
the long grass has been scythed and left lying.
Nothing is easy. The dead, whatever the living feel,
are dead.

              Even so, overflowing
our own deaths too, a tide that should be of darkness
spreads out beyond all this into shining reaches.

On the Skyline

On the skyline beyond our stream those trees,
they say, mark graves long vanished,
the stones gone to make gate-posts,
flesh and bones gone to seed, reaped.

Maybe they're all forgotten, though I doubt it.
Someone somewhere turns up a tiny box
of rusted icing (like this one here)
or photographs of legendary folk, whose traits
said to live on in child or grandchild now
emerge for good or ill in the new born.
I haven't met the people who might remember.
But these, these relics, my own history,
brown photos of the dead, the shaky outline
of 'baby's foot, aged one' (my mother's),
a pressed leaf, letters not telling much
(one even now unopened sixty years later) –
affections echoed before I lived to feel them –
these mark the secret ground of a shared life.

Looking across, how secret the change is!
My skyline echoes a strange skyline,
a churned slope up to a clump of trees
near Givenchy, nineteen-fifteen. The eyes that framed it
become my eyes, our trees look shell-blasted.
After his death in March, after the last censored
humorous teenage letters in pencil arrived,
came these photographs, his last message
to the younger sisters who'd romped with him
in trees and on rivers that nineteen-fourteen summer.

Much older than uncle was, I'm as little able
to say what I see in this skyline. But now
I do understand my mother's eye for detail,
the scarlet pimpernel, the four-leafed clover,
chestnut buds tacky in mid-winter –
things one remembers seeing a first time.
There's a shadow of communion in them, memory
makes them appear the same instead of new,

re-newed as the seasons overlay each other.
A secret language of the eye, censored
by custom if we try to speak it, links us
with the dead – their strange reticences, politics.
No odder than ours to them. That muddied hillside,
this grassy slope: a riddle seen, not solved.

Somewhere, a primitive eye may search a skyline
not unlike this one, sharing in our silence.
The blood-red hands have so long reached up
to the cave's darkness, the mother's pencil
outlined on a scrap of paper a tiny foot.

At the birth of my husband's mother, their Indian doctor,
seeing at the bedside the toddler's fistful
of strange flowers, asked, 'What has the little chap
got there?' 'I've brought daisies for my baby.'
'Then you must call her Daisy!' And they did.
Two generations later, that exchange is retold,
with love, exactly. The toddler and the doctor
are both dead, the baby well past seventy.
My stepchild Tim outlines his hand in biro.
After our deaths, those trees may catch his eye.
Affections share us, though we fail to name them.
And ground relations in more than relationship.

Resting the Ladder

Resting the ladder against the wall, I think
of the people who did this before, stripping
layer after layer of wallpaper, in all colours.
None that we like: magenta, dark green, purple.
Soon to be brilliant white. Their strange patterns
suited someone and cling, despite polycell
and water, to the knobbly walls where we
will acknowledge their permanence with a layer of woodchip,
concealing many sins. I shall be glad, though, that when
we have it as we like it, there will still be ridges
here, bumps there, to impose remembrance.

The earliest plans show Woodend at the end of a wood,
as now. Our outhouses were the farm, its water
ran from a spring through the cattle-trough to the kitchen.
There are tales of courtship between this farm and the next,
the bridge below being a meeting-place for lovers.
Sheltered, as now, in ancient hawthorns
and every winter, when snowdrifts shape themselves
again to the long-lasting land, we remember that woman
who was found frozen at the ford, her husband at war,
the baby dead up here where she's left him in safety.

Strangers drive by on the far hill ridge,
going somewhere else. For them, it is just
part of the landscape, another grey farm
with hens, horses and a lack of trees.
They will scarcely see yet the trees we planted.
A partial metamorphosis of last night's map.
Places we pass through: someone else's destination.

The ladder sways: 'We must buy a new one,'
I remind you, as we pause for coffee.
Three dogs watch our every move. The cat
whose world this is – she was born here – dozes
on my cookery books, contented in the sun.
This is no-date. This is just life. Life
as usual, as always. You are grey
with plaster-dust, and Tim writes your name
on your forehead. Now we know who you are.
The sun's moved round a little. Time to get on?

Beyond Reason

Someone who knew what dwelling means
worked out the pattern of these rooms.
We see from our cramped windows
what was first ruled on paper
by no one, a landscape
ancient, not old, and like
the rooms themselves, haphazard
and permanent, the mind
that might have created
not too evident: hints which,
beyond reason, we must
take comfort in loving.

From the moors, the dust
of summer, the snow of winter,
colour the fields yearly afresh,
the stream empties and fills
from beyond our farthest walks.
We feel welcome. This place
is unplanned for us, unlimited
by what we might have imagined.
Like us, someone stopped
on the hill ridge, and said
'here' for his few years' living.
Those who settled, with all that
that means, are dead or moved on.

Over the hill, the council estate
is laid out, dead to the world,
with views determined pen to paper,
even the trees well-planned.
The real people who live there,
our neighbours, walk this way
though there is no public right,
to raid the bushes and the stream
whose tiny illegal trout
come to fingers patient with memories.
Their children play with ours.
We learn from them the lie of our land.

In summer we will walk to pubs
at Midhope and Langsett together.

Watching, this first year, the swallow
change to a silent icicle
over the stable door,
and thinking this will be the view
of my old age, I warn myself
we shall never own this place outright.
Not only those who lived here,
but those who cross our space, seem to be
voices and figures that will supplant us.
Through them we talk with the future
which does not listen. Instead,
we listen, already we begin to listen.

POEMS OF MEMORY

1

Somewhere down the black hole
of memory, that bank of white
violets enjoys its shade, the funeral

of the boy killed on a tractor winds
through the village ('No, don't stare!'
'Why?''It's not polite.')

and up the hill the young farmer
on the pony holds his superior nose
at my donkey, in the clear spring air.

It's a friendly signal, and we go
together in the pony-trap at tea-time
to milk the cows in the far meadow.

All of nine years old, I eat my jam
sandwich in the shade, concentrating
on its crisp edges. Older than I am

by all of six years, concentrating
on the milking, my friend tilts his back
to udder after udder, and the jets swing.

That was summer. In the different dark
of a winter tea-time, the big shire,
almost on her knees, struggles to free the cart

from frozen mud, and in misplaced anger
I have grappled with my friend's whip arm.
The cart rolls back. All is to do over.

Other children. Other times. Other harm.
Not long after that, when the war
was over, I remember the hushed auditorium

of the local cinema, the sudden fear
of my father's hand over my eyes as the first
concentration-camp pictures were shown there.

Through his fingers, I saw the bodies thrust
before the bulldozer-scoop into the hole,
and a speechless survivor interviewed by the huts.

Years later, when I lifted a corrugated sheet
against a wall and found a man, bent double,
that hand over my eyes made me simply replace it.
That, and the milk's heart-beat filling the pail.

2

The knife reduces the polished oval
to mimosa on the chopping board.
Free of the shell, day-old chicks tumble

like mimosa from their box onto the floor.
Animated egg: egg sacrificed.
My mother or myself scraping the board.

Only some forty years divide
these women. Time enough for her
to die. Almost my whole life

so far. And then, how much further?
How keen and clear these seventeenth-century
broodings make each everyday pleasure,

Everywoman's task. Her hands were ugly
with domestic scars, by which I remember them now
(mine are less scarred, less gentle) most exactly.

As if on a desert island, she knew how
to make do. A harp made with string
and nails, from a fire-log, somehow

tuned to all the songs I wanted to sing
in the secret, sacred willow above the nettles,
where she pretended not to know I was hiding.

Making do. Making sacred. The magic spells
love works on coincidence. I don't need
to be told what that letter tells:

unanswerable, a friend's fatal disease.
Those chores tell it all in miniature.
And what is missing, memory supplies.

Folded, unanswered, a white blur
on the table-top, it becomes part of our home,
the sign of another marriage in our decor.

Signs in each other's lives, across time
also, though not always recognised, keep faith.
I know now that my mother used to climb

such a secret tree, pollarded, springing. Faith
with that memory helped her to let me hide
despite'Lunch ready!' (and the rest). Near-death
of a friend is now what I think of, turned aside.

3

The empty stairs from studio to studio
were frightening, even to a child.
Wide. Flat. Marble-cold.

Dark too, in the early day,
when the lights in the high well
of the stair had turned pale.

Two or three at a time, from third floor
to ground, one at a time back
with the breakfast milk, I would stop to talk

with the small man from below,
floor two (the only talkative occupant),
in his dark velvet short-coat.

Invited into his studio for tea,
with my parents, I remember he'd lift
me chest high, in affection, to eat

my biscuit while he argued theories
of painting, lifting each dark oil
with his spare arm onto the easel.

Upstairs again, my mother would turn
the taps on the gas-jets and light
the fragile gauzes, easily damaged or burnt

to a black hole. Moving the goldfish
from the table and laying the bright red
cloth for our family dinner, I wished

he wasn't down there below in a dark
I only imagined, a quiet I could not guess.
At an exhibition, the painted marks

above the long-unthought-of name
brought it all back: the slight dust over
everything, how a passing German bomber

blew my goldfish out of its bowl. I remember
all this now, but for a moment the man
below has lost his name, and only the turn

of his arm about me, lifting, is perpetual.
I dedicate that nameless memory, as I remember
the man's name, to Yankel Adler.

4

The mountains outside have folded the snow
into miles of untouched brightness. How night
seems to hover up there amongst the slow,

slow stars, while down here there is snowlight.
Now a pigeon grumbles under the archway,
disturbed, as I am, tempted to flight.

I think the squabs, born too early, may
never fledge, never fly: the skin through which
guts and eyes show blue, not likely one day

to sprout the white cloak whose magic swish
would carry them up on summer winds, rising
to a view of the mountains, tippling almost to a smash,

while the snow, untouched between us, is lying
white over the moors, and the small claw-marks
of grouse and mouse, or the rabbit's triads, fling

their delicate veins of passage between iced grasses
whose blackened blades, against the light, sway and shine.
A vein of thoughts, too, lies delicate and passes

for silence, passes like snow into the soil. Then
new life grows, and those marks vanish for ever
into the moor. Memories seep down.

The snow lies untouched between us. A clear,
black, cold night hovers above the snow.
The pigeon settles to her nest. She'll rear

her squabs after all, maybe, to tipple in the blow
of this harsh place. Love's earlier passages
rest at the root of the slow, slow

magic that a good marriage is.
New life grows. The sensitive skin,
overlaying past lives, slowly fledges.

The night and the snow hold us all, in
a giant vault. Somewhere miles away
across the untouched brightness, loves lain

to rest, with their own memories delicately vein
the distance between. You and I will wake
together, husband and wife, into our next day.

5

Jocund. Jocund after such pleasures.
The coffee is cold, interrupted by
other more urgent homely matters.

You patter back from the bathroom, innocently
naked, with a cloth and a warm towel
and a kiss, taking good care of me.

Cold coffee, then, sitting up in the jewel
the sun makes of our unmade bed,
the ruby sheets holding our smell.

Husband and wife as Van Eyck painted
in no known canvas, but might have liked to,
judging by the tender picture he made.

The hand's touch. The modest look
of true love about to happen.
The little dog not excluded. The pool

of the round mirror's limpid reflection
hung on the wall like the eye of time
approving it all, the there and then

of chance affection, like the light come
to that window-sill from far away.
Infinite space left unlit for a little room.

This and that brought us this way,
personal decisions, political events,
chances that came to seem like fate.

Like fate, too, the coming bereavements,
illness, old age, death. Often now
our present falters at presentiments.

To hold one another in the glow
of a moment's safety is the miracle
only life offers. What we know

of love, persuades that our trouble
binds us to someone's future happiness.
Our ancestors in darkness dwell

for ever, still, despite the happiness
their actions brought us to, this pool
of winter sun in which we dress.

6

Drawing the blinds, we two would romp
on all fours, wrapped in blankets,
in the dark, crying out, 'C'*est les phoques*

qui s'avancent, dit Gilbrand!' Parents
safely off somewhere, child and adult
would become seals in the wastes

of bedroom, stairs, cubby-hole, a rut
of monster beings, ourselves, pursuing
(in a dark made more familiar) . . . us . . . us!

The cries echo. Your letters are telling,
now that we are both adult, a stranger
tale, of the mind slowly exploring

its own darkness, finding a secret door
that opens between the eyes on a breaking
ice-floe. You are my nurse no longer.

Just as I didn't know the source
of that childhood phrase, I cannot know,
now, the history of these words whose force

works like magic on the dark floe
of life. The voices that made
their sense for me are gone in the undertow.

To my thoughts I welcome every shade
surviving from cave, desert, wood,
city, where those games were played.

The strange cries that change us could
be meaningless – but for that change.
In the dark night of a desperate mood

the artifice of a clarinet will change
death to life, the touch of a head
against ours, that we love, will change

beyond our physics, what goes on inside.
More meaningless still than words, these strange
messages echo between us, heard and unheard.

OPEN WAYS
September 1981

Open Ways

1 September

My father would ask me to say
why that sketch is the best
in which the line trails off into infinity
round an unfinished figure.

Underwater, against-the-light magic
of indiscernible forms.
Thoughts, too, wavering away
past the edges of perception.

Night-light, such as the Milky Way
blurs our telescopes with. Expansion,
that places the limits of it all
beyond sight, still travelling outward.

These, life-like, are open ways,
the balance of someone in mid stride.
When the year tips towards autumn
buds are beginning again.

Friends, we sit looking out
on the flow of the still fields
gold with stiff corn, brown with ploughing,
the clouds bruised and bright.

Our various lives, unfinished,
make an inner landscape.
Words dart here and there
between us, in a long twilight.

Braille

3 September

The unique self, the unique moment
again and again, irreplaceable
but born anew. He peels back
the rooty sludge he came up

coated with. I am much
too big for him. He misses
the huge watching shadow,
sees only the still grasses,

the silver meniscus flecked
with tiny flies. His eyes
bob down in the pointed skull,
rise again, glowing wet, big

with life. His fingers are shifting
over the stone, translucent, thoughtful,
like an old woman's hand on the arm
of her chair. I notice the gold

dust expanding on his skin
as he breathes. His mouth opens
on a croak that is gritty
as a puff of pollen. Stiller

than I know how, he collects himself
in the wind's ripples, his life
longer than death could ever be.
I used to think the same of my mother

half-sleeping in the sun, her fingers
restless enough to pick up the sense
of being from the chair's braille.
Shockingly vulnerable and beloved.

Ready to Leave

7 September

For Brian Walsham

Ready to leave, you suddenly talk
about the coming disaster. I notice
that the cucumber's tendrils have taken
another hitch, in these last moments.

How, my friend, should we hold in our minds
such oppositions? Young, our shock was to know
of the sun's expansion. Unemployed at fifty,
and writing poems, your generous anger

is for these young, more closely threatened,
who lock their despair into fume-filled cars,
make suicide pacts with illicit lovers,
burn themselves, after tea, on the back lawn,

plunge the carving knife to the inward pain.
Premature signs, perhaps, that the final
four-minute warning, already too late
when it will be given, is too awful to wait for.

I think the last day will be like the others.
The wonders of life, about to be dissolved,
already dissolved in our poor attention.
The truth unsaid because fashion forbids.

What duty can we, meantime, fulfil
other than that which has always been ours?
To grow with such persistent angry will
that what is to be killed is worth dying for.

On the Turn

8 September

Blurring pale on the turn,
pulsing against the tide, fanning low
over the grasses then swept away
suddenly to trace an invisible air-stream,

now blurring, pulsing, fanning again,
restless, over the sloping meadows, hour
after hour, with sharp cries but no longer
trilling to claim our land as home.

A bloom of mist has layered the woods.
In shadow the grass-blades retain a glow
of mid-morning dew. The loosened seeds
powder up under the swallows' wings.

Watching, I have stood so still that one
hovers inches from me. I am a tree
that might harbour moths or midges.
Forty line up together on the new fence

preening, flashing a buff underwing,
folding into black seeds, streamlined
by the warm south wind they face into,
guessing at the time to go. Not long,

then, before we shall be picking the green
tomatoes, drying the nasturtium pods,
getting out the gumboots, preparing again
for another climate, the swirl not of sand

but snow. A swallow takes off once more
and that throbbing curve to the spread tail-feathers,
tense as a bee-sting, as a leaping fish,
amazes as he hovers over a last few meadow-moths.

Divided

9 September

Spinning to the east, the grasses rise
against the glow, the trees are fringed
with burning, the long bulge of moorland,
divided by man, darkens again into one.

The old magic of a sun fallen away
into the earth – its light over other horizons
swelling through haze, gnawing at mountains,
dragging free of scrubland onto a flat sky.

Other bodies are lifted on the earth's bulge
to be warmed once again, while we are drawn
down on the far side, rooted to the spot
almost like any other more fixed thing,

like plants, like beasts, adapted to
wherever life finds us. Even our minds
adopt the local, the temporary, find truth
and love in what and whoever chance offers.

How other, then, all of us might be.
Even as I love this place, I detect
deserts in its grasses, jungles over the moor,
permafrost where the clay lies two feet under.

Unknown languages fret my thoughts
with alien difference, with intimate emptiness.
What names shall I give the familiar sights?
What habits do you expect of me, neighbours?

In the half-light stands my other self,
ready to kill the stranger. I see her body
wrinkle my horizon. Friend, meet me here
where we are both strangers and at home.

Signs

10 September

The fields have been stripped, the hay baled,
but the grass, silkily green again,
hasn't yet stopped growing. Our gold bars
stored in the barns are still bright,

close to, with unfaded flowers. A pile
of nettles I left for the compost crawls red
with escaping ladybirds. A late broody
fluffs her sharp breast over my palm,

lifted from addled eggs. The mealy debris
of the winter wood, which we stacked
yesterday under cover, smells of sap.
Some logs are sprouting fresh leaves.

The signs are mixed, as the feelings are.
Settling the papery hyacinths bulbs in fibre,
I hope darkness will do the trick as usual,
the spikes be firm and full by Christmas.

It is good to know we can't do everything
and have done what we can. The farm feels full,
solid with what may sustain it. The animals
are fat enough to withstand the coming cold.

Next year prepares in the borders the gloss
of crimson tulips, the mist of myosotis,
the purple crispness of the lilac's panicles,
the michaelmas daisies' white reminder.

We can and have to do nothing more.
The stab of splinters, the nettle's prickle,
the hay-fever sneeze will become the composite memory
of this and earlier and foreseen harvests.

Memories

14 September

He squinted, as if to see his memories
more clearly against the bright interference
of his garden-centre yard. His plimsolled feet
were restless. Down past the church, in his boyhood,

the cows and bulls, the shires, the pigs,
the sheep and goats would be walked in
from the villages to the big old ground
behind the town hall, now covered in houses.

His gladioli, too, would have stood unspoiled
in the show tents, if only that earlier
date had been kept to. Storm-broken beauty,
spikes flaring crimson-white, vouched for him.

Now they rise up behind my eyes all day
as new fathers and sons vie for pre-war prizes.
The fowl are spotless in their crowing rows,
udders are sponged and talcumed, bull's curls

brushed up crisply on shoulder and thigh,
coloured wools worked in the stiff tails
and spiked manes of the shimmering shires.
We are building up our own depth

of memories. Exchanging comparisons with friends –
last year, the year before, the year
before that – we avoid others whose antics
confirm a neighbourly enmity. Signs

of settling, it seems, cannot all be good.
Along with those marbled flares, I remember
his twice-repeated comment: that he liked
to see plenty of entries, whether good or bad.

About the Church

15 September

Circled about the church, horsechestnuts hang cool
in their own shade, and at noon the steps
pearl with moisture. Tablets of stone,
askew and upright, weather even here

on their windward side: the names are effaced
haphazardly, as angles and paths determine.
Soon Brownies will befriend it. For now,
the churchyard teems with more natural neglect.

Still in flower, the loosestrife has long pods
unravelling cotton-white to a spray of seeds.
Twisting, a diseased sapling grows muscular.
This year's slabs lie grassy among the monuments.

Few have bouquets, even in their first September,
though most names here take living shapes
in the shops and offices, on the hill farms.
Such a place is a cut across fibres

of continuous time. Follow any one
tombstone, it will lead through ancestral crowds
into millions – beyond civilised man, and Man,
to wordless creatures, down to the persistent

minute beings whose efforts created us.
Vegetation,too, has its ancient history,
its unchronicled struggles, its baffled instincts.
The broken fibres are bleeding a memorial mould.

Craneflies and midges, in the filtered light,
make a brilliant, zigzag dust. Of this parish
now, I wonder how far back the dead
might recognise their only lives in mine.

Double Light

17 September

At five, we're out too early. In an overcast dawn
only a finger distinguishes the tightest buds
of these mushrooms from daisies: firm, slippery,
a secretive cluster in the cropped grass.

Inquisitive, the horses come up snorting,
dewy, but warm under their tangled manes.
The cats are with us, they flit to and fro
among tussocks which the moon still whitens.

Voices to each other, we call discoveries
in the double light. I turn up my jersey
over a row of buds, but keep in hand
a few with more fragile gills, the best.

Someone must be picking too small, not trusting
to getting here before us. We have to pick,
hustled by him, smaller than we'd wish,
resenting not the trespass but that unmannerly

lack of restraint. Our anger harshens
our own exchanges, as we cover the ground
between us, disagreeing about how small
is too small, relieved when we meet to see

we have chosen the same – words and actions
imperfectly matched across the gap between us.
What reason might justify, the hand refuses,
reluctant to tear too tight a bud from the soil.

Soon, we will both be at work. Meanwhile,
there is time for walking through the dawn chorus,
talking of a future we may well be robbed of.
With no way of knowing, still we'll take our time.

POEMS BASED ON VISUAL MATERIALS

Cauldron Rituals

A prehistoric goddess-cauldron
in the Moravian Museum, Brno,
has two handles and human feet turned to one side

I

The goddess no longer carries her cauldron
on her head, or cradled in her arms. The head
and the womb have become one, mutated
to this squat pot. She sidles at you on
flat feet, little more than a stone hollowed.
Full of her triple self, possibly divine,
she waits for your choice of tipple.
Tip her up without ceremony. No riddle.
Mere clay, made by mere human.
Or open your lips to her. That wide
mouth tilted so many times to the dead
looks as if she might suck you inside-
out. Or might just as suddenly decide
to pour into you all her goddesshead.

II

In these ancient ridges you can feel
how the live clay welled up,
older still, to fit the cup
of the potter's palm, thumb and wheel
opening out, thinning the coarse pulp.
Three thousand years from that day
the clay remains barren. Whatever seed
or root might have been freed
from the soil was burned away.
Instead, big handles, twin,
with thumb-rests, look ready to make
human growth welcome. Even eyes open,
a drinker would no longer see, through wines,
or blood, those clay feet turning back.

III

From her ribs, two faces – big-eyed,
small-eared animal faces – stare
opposite ways. One looks where,
though motionless, the feet go. Backward,
the other. Neither show sorrow or fear.
Through both, one can see the world. They
themselves retain no trace of it,
absorbed in the mere looking. Fit
your fingers there, blind her, pray
now, as you drain dry this vessel –
brain, womb – that her foresight, her memory,
may not, with that same distant and double
vision, blind you to passing peril,
passing joy. Until need be.

IV

'What if, in spite of these numbers, in spite
of this glass case and the square podium,
from my navel, where the potter's thumb
pressed, a swirl of water-light
were to rise, stretching the empty womb?
An almost invisible hemisphere,
settling above the coiled stress
of gravity, engraved in my darkness
by the maker's contrary pressure.
At night, it would block my open
throat, a solid disk, quite still,
a marrowless hole in an old bone.
I am fully myself only when the moon
rounds in me her divining crystal.'

V

Making not 'cooking pot' but 'Goddess with Cauldron'.
We were still dead in our posthistory
when that special deep earth, tacky,
growthless, in keeping with long tradition
took votive form. But her hands, with memory
suddenly charged, stop as if praying
for renewal round an emptied skull
wet with blood – part the soft cradle
for a new head, birth-waters breaking.
A goddess added to this would be sacrilege.
Smiling, she makes for her secular pottery
two sturdy feet. They will carry her message,
aligned in molecules, to the moving edge
of our own, our painful, evolving prehistory.

VI

They're playing in the forest on the sliding plate
of the continent. Where others made sacrifice
to gods now dead, he turns up woodlice
under rotting debris, their legs a delicate
pale wave under the carapace.
Some he kills. Some he lets go.
She finds near the altar a horned
helmet. They scrape it out. Adorned
by turns, they chase through the reddening glow
of – is it dawn or sunset? From genesis
their atoms have sought new forms, together
spiralling between forces. Beyond this,
too, raising the reversed chalice.
On a child's head, the held may become the hearer.

Cycladic Head Haiku

For Anne Rubin

I

Head like a door-knob.
You place it on the table,
open the way down.

II

The head has no eyes.
It looks up with its whole face.
Making skies wider.

III

Once we see 'head',
we know why that blind matter
watches for something.

IV

Watchman of still earth.
If it had eyes, how much less
it would seem to see.

V

No eyes. No mouth. Nose.
Long nose, on the head's sundial.
Sniffing out the times.

VI

Was their God an egg?
All they left him of Man is
a nose for trouble.

Clay

Under clay's rim
a small sun lies,
a seed of white
in which winter dies.

Your hand has drawn,
at the point of death,
clay's memory
of a fertile earth.

Dipping to dark,
rising to light,
the clay gives birth
between day and night,

where a passage of fire
on the hardened bowl
traces the pulse
where clay meets soul.

River Form

*'To infuse the formal perfection of geometry
with the vital grace of nature. . . .'*
             – Barbara Hepworth

'A dark or a glittering drift,
or waves of spray crossing
this thin hard land,

or wind-high wetness, riving
my borders, heavy with salt,
seeping to a pale plain.'

At her dream's head-whisper, wood
longs to be lasting, calcium
hardens in the open cell.

Her hands become river, silt
their own pocked prints,
erode all marks of making.

Her dream gains the weight of centuries.
Fibre is turning to stone
round a fossil of space.

And space changes to chrysalis,
a womb filled with white fire,
dark with earth's cold.

In her last garden, space
changes again, and changes –
eye with a pupil of rain.

Swill of light in a boulder.
Movement of leaves in rock.
Held in a stone, flood-tide.

TIMESLIPS

Landfall

The sea here is heavy with silt.
The shelf has dissolved over centuries
to a heavy bronze. Pastures
eroded and broken are reaped
in graded swathes by the swoosh
of the sea's sickle.
                Trying
to make our way safer,
we look down. The grey
grains roll to admit us.

But here's a growth-knot in the smooth.

We have entered the layers
of destruction whole,
like this tender flesh turned
to stone: the gape of the shell
where a tongue of tissue calcified
to silence, its moment of sense
suspended until our senses
bent to meet it. Perhaps
on the edges of sea and land,
below the old horizon, above
the older shore, our lack
of belonging entails a right?

Passing out to sea, the shadows
of mating butterflies are holes
cut in a smooth glowing,
shafts sunk into darkness.
Above those risky soundings
the wings are twin stars
on a wobbling spindle – the gravity
of just being alive. They
are not lost.
                We belong
as much as they do, wherever
we happen. We claim the rights
only of exiles whose land

is dissolved, whose homes
and habits are beyond recovery.

Our latest language, English,
quickly erodes on contact
with incoming word-waves.
After learning *dŵr* I hear *uisge*
break on the narrow palate
of ridged sand, new soil
in the painful making.
                  They
must have heard it (their word
for water) when the wind
drove them south-east to landfall
on the lost lowlands of Wales.

In the villages rolling under
so slowly that no one knew –
symbols of eternity (burials,
monoliths) barnacled to the whale
grey of this island's weight –
did they ply their skills in safety?

Their marks have been washed
by salt or sweet water
at the river mouth, dissolved,
silted. We seldom see
(they might not recognise)
moments of theirs, important or trivial
like the hobnailed step (thinking what?)
baked into barrack brick
at Caerleon – the flesh that gave
personal weight and thought
irrecoverable now as empire.

Nemesis left just absence
to represent her, in the niche
above the killing circle.

Here, it's the soft grey
on my fingers from a layer

90

eons down this cliff that hints
how easily past might slide
over present, the heaped stacks
of history entomb us. It must be
pastures anchored to hills that hold
the land unlaunched still
on this well-oiled causeway.

                              Is that
why our fingers are so tender
over folds of stone?

                    We see
the small years of its life,
like rings in tree or crystal,
clocking pre-human time
when water fell unnamed
on the nameless ground. So wet,
hard, grainy, bright
was this place then that words
could only have silted its growth.

We like to imagine it, latecomers
with language-maps so detailed
and so different that, each moment,
the places we named have again
refused to become just home.

In a Gap of Light

Hunting on a bare rib
in a gap of light. There's danger
at either hand. Forests
set black in snow, seas
roughed over by freezing winds.
Only these mud-flats shine
slick in the sun's morning.

And the prey is there, a blackness,
stranded when the tide fell,
half the horned head sunk
in the suck.
            Now an eye turns
to the hunter's step, watches
over limbs heavy with cramp. They barely
quiver to the severing axe.

Self becomes flesh. Life
flows loosened, a red
pulse in the rising tide.
Innocent cells collapse.
Dead weight will be all that floats
free in the salt shallows.

The hunter's left a staggered
bite on the drying mud.
Thicker than blood, the silt
sifts down, a potter's slip
filling his empty steps.

Now meat smoke rises. The wolves
are uneasy. Full bellies are safe,
all the same, in a mesh of flame –
safe, as the brain transforms
flesh into dreams.
                  A match-head
glowing in a crust of skull.

What do they guess, each spring,
on the bare hill, in the ringed
nipple of stone, watching
for the seed in the cleft pillar?

Old ones have told the future
to be what it must. Their sun
obeys the spell, swings across
to a summer setting. Unseeably
floating in the pain of an open
eye, the future pulses.

Ten adult years may well
be all. And the tribe itself
is a prey to neighbours.
                        Not lost.
Nowhere to be but here,
on a dark edge moving slowly
over a molten core.

As it was in their childhood, their hills
are eternal, their shores edge
an unshifting home, their sun
sets and rises for ever.

It's the same sun that we see,
and the brain is the same. But our thought
is different: everything changes.

When the storm lifts the silt from their steps
eight thousand summers on,
the hunter's long-toed stride
clamped in the tidal flow
surprises, the mark of a strength
we forget we possess. The plod
of a beast determined to live.

Looking down the years, we read
their message: 'We walked barefoot.'

What else they passed on is here,
in our own flesh – they lived
just long enough for the seed
in the moist cell to float, a pulse of invisible change.

Now it's our turn. The hunt
in the head. Stranded on a bench
in the lab, a pale cloud
floats free of the scalpel's tip.
The cell accepts it and grows.

This flesh, this self, will be new.

And our prints, one day, may surprise it.

Nudging the Margins

The buzzard's an open throat.
A glottal stop, then a steep
fall, inflections of command.
His flight's a wide unwinding,
his barbed loops overlap
the fences at the forest edge.

He slides down the warming air
hazy over Wentwood, his underwing's
watermark comes up clear
like the sign in good paper.
But the page he is spirals
out of reach, he reverses
with a single flap, copper-plate
in sunlight, resisting intimacy.

Between his flight and the Channel's
floodtide, the veiled deciduous
glitter of wild wood
and a windless simmer, atavistic
dream-talk of neighbouring borders.

The Commission's quiver-full
of light-absorbent larches
reminds us there's nothing unchanged.

Nor was there ever.
                            The Barrage
may flood our valley floor
with a tidal flow, but the Usk's
water overcame long since
hunting-grounds older, where one
(before Stonehenge, foreseeing
nothing of this future) had stamped
a bare-footed sign of kinship.

Overlapping ways.
                            The Celts
shifted their waffle *trefs*

round the Roman legions, but still
had to fight for survival – space,
if not territory.
                    Nomadic
instinct resisted the straight
lines, the beauty of willed
order and cut stone,

harked back to those tongued oblongs,
the molten barely shaped,

those concentric rings broken
for the light to enter,

that centre whose vault would hold
the heat that makes life happen.

We think of our fences as bounds,
not borders. But from post to post
stretch crosses conceived to go deep
as tumours in the living gut,
and rays in the cell's helix
pass our more intimate edges,
explode in completed flesh,
transform the message of genesis.

A book for children has beasts
under arrows that nudge the margins,
Man at the tip of his tree.

In a barbed network of branches,
out of sight and silent, raptors
irradiate the dusk.

Dark Mothers

Gazing at shadows on a summer curtain.
Knowing that, behind, the sun is rising.

Because I am half asleep,
between me and the sun her plaster head
is a shadow watching at the sill, tilt
of nose and chin, lips opening,
a living mother come to waken.
And I am a child in cool bedclothes.

All night I've wrestled, too hot, too cold,
with old age coming fast, the brain
humming with tension on stiff shoulders.
Now everything's flowing again,
the skin eases on the blood, bones
stop drying to skeleton, are suddenly
rocks awash with gleaming salt.

Past them and out over the wave's curve
(towards where mind listens) the coo-roo-coo
of a pigeon binds me to the wild wood,
the gnarl of hollow trunks still growing.
Their pith's the film of a brain in a skull
misconceived but working. Flushes of thought
wrap in colour the scan's dark void, line
the chalice of bone whose wide eyes
can still see.
                    In mine, an after-image
of my mother's head is changing
to lines of older heritage, coiled
in uneasy dreams, where blood and bone
spiral from the sperm, spilling molecules,
shaping the changes. The sun is young
that saw them beginning. It casts an image
on our drawn blinds – the Dark Mother
of past and future jungles. The tilt
of her brain lifts blind eyes
to horizons invisible.

                    No straight line
draws us beyond the coming deaths,
humankind's, the earth's, our own,
but – as the human hand illuminates
spirals from leaf through word to nondescript –
the sun could craft a becoming, our branch
arrowed from life-tree to open margin.

Just now, a mere half-century holds me
woven into sun and shade, half dreaming
under open windows. There is a chorus
of shorter lives, buzzing and chirping shadows,
a silent drift of butterflies and leaves
and, seeking entry at the curtain's slit,
ginger mog, my angular black Anubis.

Solstice

In a double bank of brambles
bared at the winter solstice,
obstructing, defining a path from
our mossy gate to the forest,
all seasons have grown together.

Knob of sodden berry,
burnt out death's head,
flesh crumpled to the skull.

Tight green cobble,
ready for the summer coming
on the far side of winter.

Clasp of pink petals
over a mound of yellow,
pips pushing up pollen.

And many-eyed ripeness,
sacs of ruddy juice
round the pale boats.

All these are hidden now.
Where yesterday we went in mud
I walk an untrodden place
under tossed branches, between banks
of bouncing brightness, the sun
dazed with snow just fallen.

Paper. No pen! To mark
the words' beginning, might I
move a leaf, a twig, a stone?
Or let thought's memorial be
traces in the cells, lighter
than snow, more lasting perhaps
than messages in pollen?
                              Distant,
the minds that made us. Sacred,
our present, to their memory, the press
of desire in us for futures.

'Bleep-bleep, bleep-bleep.' Electronic pulse
of bird-sound, hidden in a web
of bare branches. 'Bleep-bleep',
invisible in corridors of sap
at the flawed edge of the air,
black traceries, veins, nerve-ends.

At my feet an ash-twig, powdered
with green decay. If I hold it
like a drawing-tool, will it smear
enough of up or down stroke?

The bird is silent now,
knowing I've seen her, leaf-veined,
brown among brown leaves,
flying ahead of me ankle-high,
slipping soundless through facets
of emptied space, resting
on bones she has known all summer.

She's a hacking brown flint
that stops and starts in my path.

She is making me her poem.
A stag, delicate and cloven,
breaking the snow for her sake.
Or, since she stays ahead,
what I am, two-footed beast
with food maybe, further on.
A beast in wellies.
                    My fingers
are green with mould or lichen,
a strange pollen, this ash-tip
a dinosaur's three-toed tread
blurring and blunting my words.
They will take deciphering. As if
I had written in the dark, at school,
criss-cross, after lights out,
to my left-hand fingertips, keeping
the lines clear.
                    Now the bird

calls once more, disappointed
when I turn for home. Or claiming
my prints as her larder till snow,
falling again, fills them.

      Whiteness breaks
into flurries at this branched margin,
and the only green things now
ancient knotched mares'-tails,
confusing the track's edge,
too fine, too hard to be settled on.

My page too will allow
no more. It is wet with crystals
which my hand's blood crumpled.

Snow thickens over the brambles,
their multiple seasons. On the wire
at the farm's edge, where our gate
mosses in the forest's breath,
flakes have become dew
flicked by the wind, buds,
nail-tip up-ending lenses.

In my pocket, predatory triumphs,
happenings of vowel and consonant,
cells of an evolving tongue.
My leaves, twigs, stones.

Quarry

The long lines of their edges
interlace in the haze, bare
masses of sandstone, clouds
of rock.
   The scoop of glaciers
is nothing here. Yesterday
they melted. It is desert one feels
under the short brown grass. The surprise,
to find, broken off in mid air,
solid rivers – the silted lenses,
the sense of invisible sources.

In this quarry, a group of us stand
below the earliest of plants,
black strands of life,
spore-heads in the stone.
On this ground, our forebears
never set foot. The worst,
and more than the worst, might already
have happened: nothing but elements,
heatings and freezings, continents
adrift, breaking.
     But in rock
at our feet, fine-grained as flesh,
is the swirl of a single wave.

How the sun flows over it, a flutter
of gold in the summer air.
It would have been beautiful, that fine
film of clear water.

Not hard to believe. But eyes
were not made then. Millennia
were still to align the molecules
in striations of ice.
     We are early
humans, between glaciations, trying
to see. Cities are suddenly
myths we barely remember.

More real, these fibres, enlarged
for our straining eyes and angled
to catch how daylight fell,
once, on their ribs and knotches.

We are grateful to see this, life
leaving its mark in the silent
upheavals. But the layer that will hold
us may be thinner, with black
deposits sealing it, and graves
of our kind inexplicably massed.

Instructed to test the rock
for silt or mud, we crumble
pieces in our teeth. It is mudstone,
smooth, without taste. The river
flows again, thickening, messageless
on our tongues.
                    There is time
for it all to happen again.

Or not.

            A drift of seed
hesitates in the quarry mouth
meeting the still cold.
Light catches it.
                    As I watch,
my brain is an estuary, shallow,
dazzled with plankton, cells
at the tide's mercy, idling.

Matter watching itself.

Winged As They Are

A ragged canopy over cold
and broken water. The light
is above the leaves, behind
their three-pointed mirk, the silent
slide and lift.
                    Pull down.
On the underside, small flies
each angled to a hard vein,
the nearest. Facing the stem.

Turn the leaf over. One walks,
stately, on invisible legs,
with knees the light just thickens.
Another shifts off tetchily,
keeping its wingspread distance.
Now several move. First
they sidle, fan out all the way
to the spiked edges. Then they swing
over and down, to where the shade is
a shade deeper. Their napes are pale,
their see-through wings are folded,
a dark nib, as they arc
across acres beyond – the seething
sunshine of uncut pastures
(what heads of floating yarrow)
between leaf-shade and root-shade.

Backs to the edges of the air,
they must surely be conscious, winged
as they are, of the sycamore's corridor,
the swaying, windy dark. Their leaf
hangs in and helps to make it.

Let go, it flips face up and rises
on its branch. Sure-footed, they sidle back.
You can still see them against the light.

Borders

The frog is an ochre echo
of the JCB above us.
                    His world's
compacted to a rot of darkness,
the soft pale stalks
of wetland grass, where his paths
ran hidden, jumbled and banked
high now over deep water.

A male, neat, big-eyed,
hard, how he burns now
in my tightened fingers, thrusts through,
almost, between bones, the mucus
of home still coating his hardness.

Where there's water undisturbed, I kneel
to the edge. He hesitates, then dives
to a new world. Kicks up,
bobs, puffing too hard.
His hands cling to the fronds.
Water slopes from him
in a glittering collar. Ring
after ring flows from the beat
of his gasping, brings back
the shape of strange borders.
But the legs dangle, flaccid,
wavering.
              Dying?
                    All at once
he strikes out, splay-footed.
Is gone. The surface settles.

Maybe, from under the stone
I place for him here, he'll send out
at sunset, next breeding season,
a cry to remind us of dinosaurs,
loud over the skin of water,
claiming it, while their vast lake
slowly tips between Gwent and Somerset.

But a part of him was before them,
between delicate thighs creeping
from one puddle to the next.

Drawing Breath

Hooked by their long knotched legs,
they stand on these bouncing panicles.

Within the shifting glow,
the faceted mounds of their eyes,
I must be recorded, a safe
unimportant stillness in this angled
opening and closing of wings.
Edges of shade, self-cast,
interrupt the sun, triangles
of beating unsteady darkness.
When they fall wide open,
a dying light catches
in the mammoth-red of their fur.

A summer wind from the east
ruffles it with hints of ice.

Glaciers. There were once here,
pressing, releasing the land
through the short pulse of our time.
A wave, travelling beneath us,
is dropping the crust to the sea.
Where an ice-age may meet it.

The buddleia's weighty sprays
seem to draw breath. Nuptial
butterflies tumble among swallows,
wobble down to feed. One is wafted,
rustling, to the page, tests it.
Her trunk is a hair-spring
uncoiling, tasting the whiteness.

She has reached the end of her changes.

But as she explores these pits,
these bumps, the residue of trees,
I glimpse her descendants, sucking
traces from the face of ice-floes,
finding cracks of climate to weld
their tight-ribbed eggs to.

Timeslips

The swifts let fall their shadows
in hazy brilliance, their flight
as high as it will be over Africa.

My book shows a ridge zigzagging
blackly across desert: an ice-age
dropped there its gritty melt-waters.
Leaving the Sahara liquid
with greening shallows. But now
sand shimmers, casting up
only timeslips of water.
                            That's where
they are going, those birds, while my mind
migrates through damp grass, downward.

Sands of equatorial Wales
stretch there, forgotten in darkness.

My layer of climate thins
to a bloom of lichen. Meaningless.
Like the dot at the tip of my pen
which needs the page's memory
to give it its place in a word.

This land will be covered over
and our bones with it, fossils
that may not be found, nor given
a place in the species' history.

Neanderthal's larger brain
makes me fear my own in its cave
of bone. Space behind the eyes,
where the swifts swoop among trails
of uncertain thought, among words
whose alternatives must be jettisoned
to make a sentence.
                            Alternatives
that stutter a desert image –
boy-child starving in the lap

of his mother, the perfect feet
that will never feel the ground, the wrinkled
buttocks that will not become those
of a man, the open mouth
behind which a brain is obliterated.

They might be that first couple,
Mother and Child of us all,
mirage of them, icon
in the air, hovering over fossil
footprints, a black madonna.

Which two million years will not save.

At sunfall, among the swifts,
noctules. Still finding their way
by echoes. After fifty million.

Natural History

Engraved to fit the brain, just three
bones are what's left of her, 'Swanscombe Man'.
I feel for the supra-iniac fossa,
sign of otherness, of being Neanderthal.

Sensings and thinkings, of a kind now lost
(and forever), warmed this neat round jigsaw –
a mass of existence real as bone.

My fingers are drawn back and back
to the dent in the skull, as if her fingers
remembered, through me, what it is to live.
As if I could hear her hair rustle,
intimate, through my own head-bones.

At my shoulder, a girl cries 'Ugh!
How disgusting!', shrilly laughs and grabs her man
by the naked arm. Their bright reflections
place them, for a moment, in the glass cases.
Then they are gone, echoing on the stair.

This death was more real to her than to me,
the dirty transformation we know, and know of,
in homes and on borders. The honoured. The dispossessed.
I raise my hand to my head, seeming
to feel what's impossible, the hollow sign
of different being.
                        This labelled cave
is alien. Empty, like her three curved bones,
of the real existence of consciousness. Which left
no evidence, till words were fossilised in stone,
or ink drawn fragile over skins or printed
on destroyed forests. Museum-shelves of libraries.
Coal-faces of our own uncertain future.

Standing here, I see my head float
behind the skull, in a dark wet window
starred like a night sky, with drops
jerkily falling, driven by blusters

to invisible sideways paths or stops
in the smooth, slowly-moving glass.
                                        I think
of the earth's surfaces, riding and dipping.
Ice-ages and deserts and seas that will come.

Not everything's possible. How to tell though
what will matter? Movements of the mind,
unwitnessed even, do leave traces
for thought to run in. DNA of a self
taking flesh, to change us, in look or language.

The ridged brow in front of me leans
empty of all futures. So hard, even now,
to imagine ourselves what we really are.

Leaving past the cases, there's a flicker of me,
ghost in a train window, far out.

I think of the lovers.
                        Imagine him cupping
her tilted head.
                        Feel the forehead on th

WORDS FOR MUSIC

Commissioned by the composer Geoffrey Palmer

If Mind Remember

1

Cat on a silver lawn,
dew-drops on hunting feet,
eyes green as the dawn
rising through woodland light.

Fur is a living shade
open to that inner glow.
Through her eyes the green world
looks up at a misty window.

2

A forehead burning
on the chill glass.
Will the pain pass,
love not returning?

Look, on grey grass,
the hunter's passing –
run, pause and spring.
Love too may pass.

But better, better
if mind remember.
The deepening ground:
love lost, love found.

3

Traces of human feet
leaving across the lawn.
Dew holds in the dawn
fossils of rising light.

Beings in daylight's glow
long for the dreaming shade.
Light, dark make the world.
Throw wide a morning window.

A Trace Known

1

In the muffled sea
of the forest, something
has brought you to me
as you used to be.

That far sunny fling
of branches or, below,
these roots, thrumming
in shade, but holding?

All those years ago
you stood somewhere
like this, in a flow
of light and shadow.

And now you are here
where you've never been,
and I suddenly fear
you, like a new lover.

2

Here, where you've never been,
you stand in silence, as though
unsure of me, dearly uncertain
as you were then,
when neither of us could know.

How exactly yourself you are,
like a dream or a memory.
And I, I inhale in the dark
pine-sap sharpness
of you standing near me.

O those years! The moving miles
of the forest, its ever-green loosed
secretly, needle by needle, while
in us each cell
we knew each other by was lost!

3

You seem as you were when you
came to me, love's first day.
Together we stood by a grey
sea, when suddenly the light
rippled, breaking at our feet,
and I turned to speak to you.

'Look how bright the water is
as it comes to us' – touch by touch
and, at the edge, each
wave lifting to show,
as it broke, in the undertow,
small fish feeding in flurries.

You said what you saw were black
bars coming to us, one
by one from the white sun
burning at the centre, shadows
of wind battering the shallows.
But you did not draw back.

4

No right of mine
to help or hold.
You must grow old
beyond my mind,
lost in a fold
of time's cold.

But what you were
no time can change,
a single creature
brave and strange –
one like no other
kinder, nearer.

Time sinks away
like a fold of stone,
and we alone
recall the day
when a touch, grown
into love, could cancel
past, future, all
we would know, or had known.

5

Hardly moving, the warm air
of the forest is a tide of sound
with only, here and there,
a trace known
by its origin.

Bird bounce, fox rustle, wing clap,
alarm trailing over distant ground,
then, at my ear,
seep of water, creak of twig, rise of sap

and, under it all,
invisible, the great stone shelves,
traces of deaths and lives
breaking again into soil.

Esther

Verse libretto for twenty-minute opera in a single scene.

Set

The Palace at Susa, fourth century BC.

A single scene: semi-circular backdrop in broad planes of white and violet, the royal colours, providing a series of 'pillars' behind which we see Esther pass from time to time, as the text indicates.

Mid-stage, on a raised dais, there is the ceremonial throne of King Xerxes, with above it the winged disk, emblem of Ahura Mazda.

When the action begins, the throne is in darkness so that King Xerxes, already seated, cannot be seen.

Characters

Esther/Hadassah, Queen of the Persians, a Jew. *Soprano.*
Haman, Chancellor of Persia. *Tenor.*
Xerxes, King of the Persians. *Bass.*

The names Hadassah and Haman are stressed on the last syllable.

Stage in darkness.
Esther enters, spot-lit, stage left, wearing a cloak of gold cloth. She walks centre stage, throws the cloak to the ground. She is now dressed in a simple dark robe.

ESTHER　How can I wear them now, those robes that make
a Queen of me? Xerxes the King, my lord,
my love, has ordered that the Jews be killed
throughout his kingdom. Deserts, valleys, hills
must be made clean of them. When plots were made
against the King, the Jews it was who brought
the news to me. And I, I am a Jew.
Disguised, I lived here and may live so still,
wrapped in these shining folds as in the love
of Xerxes, if I keep my secret close.
But, to be Queen over this massacre!

120

She prays. Well-spring of all things, hidden deep
within my soul – however changed
my soul may be since first I heard
Thy secret murmur – lift me now
so strongly, sweetly, that my death
will seem a bubble on the tide.
I break, into Thy moving wave.
I lose and find myself in Thee.

*Esther gathers up her cloak and exits left. However she can be seen
passing, from time to time, behind the pillars. As she moves, she
again robes herself as Queen for her confrontation with Xerxes.
During the following scene, Esther's thoughts are intermittently
overheard.*

ESTHER   Haman, whose heart is full of pride and fear
they go together – poisons the King's mind
with tales of hidden danger from the Jews.
The King accepts his word and has decreed
a massacre. You do not know, O Xerxes,
by this you will destroy our love, and life
itself for me. No, I'll confess the truth
to save my people. And if I perish, I perish.

*The lights have come slowly up, revealing Xerxes, in ceremonial robes.
From centre stage, Haman is approaching the steps of the throne.*

XERXES   Haman, second in rank to ourselves, prudent
above all other councillors, approach
your King, advise us honestly. All night,
since to this edict we have set our seal,
doubts have disturbed our dreams. We seemed to see,
as if from high above, our sleeping towns.
The roofs, transparent to us, show the babes
in their mothers' arms, lovers in gentle sleep,
young men whose vigour might enhance our state,
old men whose blameless lives should end in peace. . . .
Haman, it seemed to us these were the Jews!
And, waking, we remembered how it was
the vigilance of the Jews protected us,
our throne and our authority. Speak then
before your Lord. What should prevent our hand
withdrawing from this act? Speak fearlessly.

HAMAN   As ever, mighty Xerxes, King of Kings
is moderate. His will is to provide
for all his loyal subjects, peace, a life
forever steady, with no doubt, no change,
if they will keep the law, emblem on earth
of that eternal truth which rules the skies.
My Lord, you bid me speak. The Jews are not
such people. They believe their God requires
continuous change – as if the universe
were a great desert! Ever-shifting paths
traverse the sand and then are gone. How can
nomadic people understand our laws?

XERXES   Law is the greatest good. If law may be
assured only by death, then my decree
must stand. Have the thing done. Have the thing done,
but do it quickly. Not a single one
must live to weep or to remember. Go.
Establish peace for ever here below.

*Haman backs away from the throne. However, before he can quit the
stage, he pauses, having caught sight of Esther behind the throne,
stage right, now in full regalia. He overhears what follows.*

Xerxes thinks himself alone.

XERXES   With certainty, I feel my power returns
and, like a thunderbolt, my sceptre burns.
Throughout my lands the loyal people cry.
Their King must act, and all the Jews must die.

ESTHER   God of our fathers! Help us!

XERXES   Woman, you dare!
Not even a Queen may come unsummoned here!
On pain of death, go hence.

ESTHER   My Lord! My Love!
I come in desperation.

Xerxes rises, moves threateningly towards her.

See I fall

before you. Hear me. Hear me in your heart!
Do not destroy me, let me speak. I am
a woman you have loved. My Lord! My Lord!
You stand before me as the angel of death.

XERXES What is the matter, Esther? Come to me.
I am your brother. Take heart. Do not die.
Come to me, speak. I am a man again.

Xerxes gathers Esther in his arms.

ESTHER My love, my Lord . . . My name is Hadassah,
not Esther. Let me tell the truth, my love,
now, in your arms, then let me die. My name
is Hadassah, not Esther. I was not named
after a star, remote in the night sky.
My emblem is the myrtle, ever-green,
set in the sandy soil, the flowers white,
spicing the desert air. I am a Jew.

Esther loses consciousness.

HAMAN A Jew! What will become of me.

XERXES A Jew!
And yet, she brought me news that saved my life.
She seems as if already dead. She lies
abandoned in my arms, as she has lain
in love. And yet, I know, I know her now,
as I have known no other. O the taste
of her is in my soul. My Hadassah!
My Hadassah! I was your conqueror.
My ways were alien to you, yet you loved,
you saved, you cherished me.

HAMAN Concealment! Lies!
What guilt was this? What plot? I blame myself.
To think these people came so near my King!

Becoming aware of Haman, Xerxes rises.

123

HAMAN   A woman is a woman. But the State,
            the State is truth on earth, and you its God –
            unhesitating will, unchanging Law.
            No man may question what you have decreed.

Esther regains consciousness as Haman, gesturing towards her, continues:

HAMAN   The Jews must die. This is their plot, my Lord.

ESTHER   O then despair, despair, my people! Death,
            death by the sword, blood in the desert sand.

She rises, distracted.

            No! No! Haman must die, he and his sons,
            his wife, his kin, all that support his cause.
            Let them be killed! Let them be hung on high
            from the great walls of Susa! Let their flesh
            fall from their bones into the mouths of dogs.

XERXES   Haman, her gentle soul, I have destroyed it.

HAMAN   O now she speaks with her true voice, my Lord!

Xerxes takes up a commanding position before the throne.

XERXES   Go hence. I hear in what you both have said
            truths. Different truths. You wish each other dead.
            I wish you both to live.

Esther and Haman exit separately left.

                         My task should be
            to force a truce. My power might set them free.

Xerxes seats himself on the throne.

            Once, when in distant lands I still could pass
            unrecognised, a peasant woman, old
            with toil before her time, told me, 'My boy,
            the ear is where intelligence resides!

124

Listen and you will learn.' That night the floods
between conflicting rivers broke her strips,
her seams of husbandry. 'You see,' she said,
'Each river changes course, but both build up
the land that grows between.' The fertile mess,
as the sun rose over the gulf, shone gold
between the rivers' arms. And out to sea,
as the years passed, new land has come to be.

*Off-stage, the voices of Esther and Haman can be heard in
altercation as Xerxes rises and steps forward to make his decision.*

HAMAN We do not want your people. Everywhere
you spread new thoughts, new manners, infiltrate
our institutions, till we feel that we
are strangers to our own, our ancient ways.

ESTHER What right have you to speak for Persia? You
stranger yourself! The lure of ancient ways
has weakened many nations.

HAMAN   Silence! You
have been a traitor even to your own race –
denied your people for a royal bed.

XERXES That vision has been with me from my youth.
But I have learnt, as King, a bitter truth,
faction is power. My role, to make a choice,
since few will grant their enemy a voice.
Haman or Hadassah, old ways or new.
The choice is false, but love at least is true.
Love leads to change, it opens strangers hearts.
Haman must die. So the dream of peace departs.

THE END

VAUGHAN VARIATIONS

'. . . make these mountains flow,
These mountains of cold ice in me.'
– 'Love-Sick'

1

> '. . . that's best
> Which is not fixed, but flies and flows . . .'
> – 'Affliction'

Broken across 'sepulchrum' and
'voluit', your stone is perhaps,
after all, as you would have wanted:
needing to be sought out, letters
(though legible) well greened over,
and the eye drawn away to where,
against the light, dispositions
dear to you are being restored,
things short-lived steeped in dusk, edge-lit –
a heap of eastward-facing ground,
and below (what's hardest to change)
falling water between mountains
whose high heads throw moving shadows
to tell time, emptying the fields.

These you could foresee, spaces that
would remain (that will remain) longest.
And in plain fact, perhaps nearby,
there's matter that held you, and still
lives on. But never you again.
At other times, I've looked for you
in your language, shapes that you'd own
traced by words that change and die off.

I see here how your voice and his
might evolve their ways. Toddler-talk
of twins, down by that clear amber,
half drowned in its hushed and hushing,
the soft pour of those melting pleats –
made and remade, same shapings in
changing water. Your mother's tongue,
then English, making, remaking.
Swirled by what can't be said. All this,
near your grave, has made you too real,
like a parent after his death.

My temples ache as if with tears.
It's a betrayal to say 'you'
to the self your words breathe in me.

2

'Who empties thus will bring more in.'
— 'The True Christmas'

He would not have us think of green
in mid winter, but face the cold —
without metaphors of springtime
to deck the house, without more hope
than a child can give, being born
in poverty and in danger.

From Sarajevo, a man's voice,
all its tones reduced to flatness,
tells how he saw the baby girl,
her head covered in blood, a hole
the size of a ten-pence piece in
her forehead. And she was alive.
A doctor was trying to clean
the nose, the mouth, the eyes, the ears.
Outside, her mother waited, the
breast of her blouse red. Her husband
had been killed in the early days,
and her sister in law, to help,
was baby-sitting when the shell
broke through the wall of the kitchen.
An official bent to tell her
that her sister in law was dead,
adding 'but she died instantly'.
Then, crying too, he knelt to pray.

I have no prayers for the dead
or the living. I wish I could
think of more than of taking aim
from the snowy hillside, and of
sitting or standing in that room
while the shell uses the law of
physics to pass from me to me.

130

I seem to see you, poet
who had fought in a civil war,
doctor on edge with winter deaths,
taking your pen at Christmas time –
impatient, starting a poem
'So stick up ivy . . .' – a candle
perhaps still burning by your hand
and the 'warm snow' of your wife's breast
still near enough to be evoked
strewn with red roses, as image
for unseasonal frippery.
'Green will remind you of the spring . . .'
Instead, better to know the earth
as it is at the deadest time.
The page slowly filling with thought.

No way of foreseeing us. His
hope or despair are of his time,
snow drifting on the valley paths
which his cob will take, sure-footed,
to the next bedside, death or birth.
Where skills other than medical
will be needed, a heart well-tried
and everyday words of comfort.

May he discover, as he rides,
the clean grey branches of the ash
preparing their black buds, and in
a sheltered covert those hanging
dashes of hazel, loosening,
as they do now. Something we can't
stop, or bring on. Not metaphors.

'Give thy soul leave.'
– 'Rules and Lessons'

I invented it, so why
since then, do I see your hand
come of its own accord to the mind's eye?
How must I understand
the precision of its placing there?
The candle is beyond,
as I first wrote, and a short shadow
nudges the page when the flame gutters.
To the left, pale squares: a window.
Closer, the dark is shapely, stirs
at sunrise with things that are things you know,
or would be, if you were sitting here.

Is that it? The hand's not mine,
but it lies where I see the triangle
of my own hand travel after the moving pen
and stop, hunched ready. Invisible,
the where-you-were, because I am here.
This is the space, then,
imagination would have me know.
The space that tastes of self. Uneasy
at the trespass (now I find it so)
I turn the words and let them take me
to my own hand. A double shadow
patterns half-written thoughts, shed there.

No candle now in the grey dawn
but a bulb. It's at this hour
your heart's events, genesis, restoration,
come, though in new terms, nearer.
How I need your frankness here!
A stuttering permission
(though all the *but's* crowd in) to praise.
Standing at the window, I hear you say
quietly, 'Mornings are mysteries.'
Despite the disgraces that mark our century,
still the page calls for difficult honesties.
And would pass them on, from here to there.

4

'. . . hieroglyphics quite dismembered . . .'
  – 'Vanity of Spirit'

Before I drew them, the curtains were pale
with snow where, in the square window, the bank
rises out of sight to the gutter's edge.

The green that is usually there (that I
seldom notice) I sense now, its darkening
of the white, private folds of the linen.

I criss-cross newspaper spills (whose headlines,
before they flare up, catch the eye briefly),
jigsaw the coals, reach down to set the match.

The double-glazing is a wall of light.
Behind me, the flames flap like spring washing.
The snowflakes are big, slow apple-petals.

It's the edge of middle-Europe's blizzard.
We saw it last night, wrapping silent guns,
smoothing in the rubble slides for children.

Hanging close enough to knock with their wings,
a twirl of siskins ravels, unravels
as I move about in here behind glass.

The phone rings – a bit of good news – but still,
behind the eye, TV pictures flicker
as they always do when one turns away.

A shaft of sun, levelled from under cloud,
strikes without warmth and on the chimney breast
the peanuts are a cylinder of shade.

While it lasts, grey silences more rapid
than the eye can catch (to name) are making free
within hand's reach. But they'd slip my fingers.

5

'Dead I was, and deep in trouble.'
 – 'The Holy Communion'

The hillside's a fall of water –
loud, late-spring shower
dropping warm light
from leaf to leaf.
Bright sprays of beech
drop shadow, dots of it,
onto the dry grit road.
At the edge, there's a shine of ivy,
its pale downy new tips
feeling out for firm ground.

Why do they draw me so?
After months in the this and that,
hardly trying to live as joy
can let you, I'm grit dry.
Through love, was his way. To a sense
of God. Attention becoming prayer.
Only his mind's movement,
flung beyond circumstance, traced
in changed words, is left me.
The gesture's wordless message.

After the rain, the path's a shade
less dry, and my mare's neck
and my jersey and the path itself
steam, a grey warmth rising
on all sides, like breath.
On the trochees of her walking hoof-beats
vowels and consonants of the forest
improvise their almost-silences.

What I don't know how to make words of
seems to be said all around me.
I copy what I can. Images.
Taking advantage. The rest
works on untainted. Still distant.

6

'. . . *sense*
Things distant doth unite . . .'
        – 'Sure, there's a tie of bodies'

By a slant in the self
that
    between layers
                of real things
finds real things

nuclei   their held spaces –

not to think about   to be
to know
(but only afterwards   only to know you've known)

to ebb
        then
                into a single place
(you can see it in the mirror)
a dying place

and be astonished

a terror of limitation
your intimate home
                now the trap of death.

How you need it
                something to point the self at   (to remake it)

something offered
                you have no responsibility for it
                it is a miracle of indifference

                light on the edge of a leaf

to love it

and then
        after all
                to have been there too.

7

For Tony Connor

'Accept this salmon caught in the rushing weir . . .
How safely he could have lain hidden in those still pools!'
— translated from De Salmone.

Having fished the Usk for a salmon,
Henry sent it to Thomas Powell.
But your gift, Tony, is of our times.
On this salmon, I'll not burn my thumb!

Tender between ripples of plastic
which, as I lift them, glitter with grease
(packed in a Scotland that was only,
in the life of this fish, a trade name
for squared-off paddocks of H_2O)
it's a gift between poets still, hint
of what both might be hoping to catch.

I surround it with salad, pour wine
(rosy as peat-water over stone).
We talk politics, not poetry,
which makes me think of Henry's old friend
unfolding those crafty Latin lines
(that smelt a bit, maybe, of fresh fish),
knowing what 'still pools' were really meant.

Fellow-prisoners at one time, they both
would feel a right, a duty even,
to honour the dead by living well –
'discreet joys' of friendship, deeper ones
that were, that are, better not spoken of.
What isn't said, or written, we both
'secretly reflect', being old friends.

The chill-pack came out of your pocket
without a poem, but like one – palmed
between us, unsureness on both sides.

The more I read, the wiser it gets.

8

'Hath flesh no softness now? Mid-day no light?'
– 'The Tempest'

I thought my mind's eye would have seen them,
the twins, aware of their own times
as they drew up at the Watton Gate,
with Brecon's walls on either side –
somewhat as I remember Dover,
the harbour-arms and the white cliffs,
grown-ups confident of safety there
while, behind us, German armies
gathered to fan out over Europe.
Even before the Civil War
living near those turrets must, for them,
have made conflict something quite real,
like jets too low over this valley.
Now there is one small heap of stones
by the Borough Council's thin prefabs,
to one side of an open road.

When I did see them, it wasn't there
but watching two noisy lads play
under Tal-y-Bont's wild waterfall
a short ramble from Newton Farm.
One brother, bare already, the pool
amber up to his raised elbows.
The other, much the same age, stretching
a hand, as if to pull him out.

But conspirators, they are, as boots
inch downward on wet, sloping stone!
Now, on dry rock, all their clothes stiffen.

Each feels a ring round his chest, like
the mouth of a fish, the scales flashing
to fire under his beating palms.
From the ledge above, new water comes,
a cold breath of white sound falling.
But where they are, it's *igne tincta*,
water 'tinged with fire'. Origins.

What, in this century, can be made
in language, not to deny this?
When, through that small bright window at home,
they've already seen more violence
than Henry and Thomas as grown men?

I look on them as they may look
back. From outside. Mostly with the eye.
To which their naked whiteness breaks
into streaks and wobbles of wet light.

Something the human eye stares at.

9

In the ninth year since my father's burial.

'Nothing that is, or lives,
But hath his quickenings, and reprieves.'
     – 'The Holy Communion'

I wanted words (needed and lacked them)
then and, for this, ever since he died.
No lies, but no truths either, beside
that grave. Just a box-hedge emblem,
evergreen, marking off the hectare, denial
of what the countryside flamed with – stubble
stretching all round the churchless graveyard.
A dark oblong, a bowless barge, a hard
stillness on that swell of bright lines closing
toward flat horizons on every side.

The wife (widow), the daughter, tongue-tied,
watched the lowering with straps, the lengthening
with spades, the lowering again of the body
in that mis-measured coffin. All done silently.

What I thought then, I can'ßt remember.
Less too big, I know, than too small
the coffin seemed, for all that was in there.

Then a man, in there, suddenly was all.

I see his last works as broken faces,
criss-crossed human landscape, with lines that
strike the edge, aiming for spaces
beyond, dimensions the bright flat
map of a canvas can only hint at.
And yet the mouth and eyes are never
offset, but full-face to the viewer,
central, as though (from the sliding places
each comes from, and is part of) a look, a word,
face to face, may be met with, heard.
No false sentiment there. It's all just
paint, with no personal brush-stroke. Dead.
As the man who put his life into it is dust.
Cold as the Celtic cult of the head.
All the more precious, those human traces.

'Comment ferais-tu ça en poesie?'
me demandait-il, of some technical trick
that was always more – a formal magic
not against but beyond thought, like music
or the way words work with silence in poetry.

This ninth autumn, corn-cobs grow fat, ripen –
vertical green yaffles! Echoes reminding of childhood.
Winged laughter in Somerset orchards, war not much more
        than
fuselage in a field. And between two languages, understood
as a child understands, gaps in too-human vision.

In Belgium, where I might have lived, tractors will already
have cut the tall maize flags and the still cemetery
will seem to float again on that vast sea-soil.

It's not the father that comes to mind but the youth
crouching in Brussels, as he told me, with a shark's tooth.
Out of his depth in a more-than-social turmoil.

10

'What emanations
Quick vibrations
And bright stars are there?'
– 'Midnight'

Midday.

The sheep lie
on the high ground.

This is their habit,
to seek a vantage
before they sleep.

The hills from this height,
and the valley, look shadowless,
as if light from within
had replaced the sun.

Surfaces familiar,
lovely, of home,
lose definition.
The skin no longer
limits or touches.

It seems. It seems
a rolling meniscus,
holding only just.
Pressed between different
densities. Fragile
immense location.

Of which awareness
comes as it is broken.
Weight returns.
The thin circle
of grass-blade and shadow
on a stone by my head
trembles a little.

Nothing to be afraid of.
I can smell the warm
ewe's wool as a lamb
butts and suckles.
For me too
a place waits
in which love can be
natural as death.

And better it is
for that other, though what
that other may be
formula and word
both fail. It is
like a breath, like
eating and drinking are
(extensions of matter).
Like making love.

How could Henry believe
that an orphan lad
shepherding on the mountain
saw a youth garlanded
in green? Who loosed
a hawk (as he slept)
which flew through his mouth
to his inward parts,
so he woke gifted
with fear and poetry.

11

'. . . who did thee bring
And here, without my knowledge, placed,
Till thou didst grow and get a wing.
A wing with eyes, and eyes that taste?'
– 'The Query'

He didn't deny them, the contradictions,
the twists of mind and mood, the boring
et ceteras, the grit between visions,
and the visions themselves, unaccountable,
unearned, hard to own up to.
Because of war, imperfection, change.

He would work, to heal himself
and others, with words or herbs.

That day, at his desk, as often
(to write poems, to write prescriptions),
his hand hesitates. How shall he,
so questioned about the Bards,
return a worthy answer?
The man who asks will read
in a noise of hooves, wheels
and street-cries, polluted air,
new books on a busy table.
This page under his wrist,
when written, will be just a
footnote on ancient things,
on old fogy's last words.

Not often I see him smiling
but I do now. His eyes travel
from his new window to those hills
that lie one within the other
in a haze of autumn brilliance.
Sometimes the inner (the smaller)
is bright, sometimes a dark blot.
Like his own soul, he thinks,
drawing breath at the sensed entrance
so near now. Down by the glowing clarity

in the foreground, a swan he's fed
at his back door paddles
on its own shade, like an apparition.

Something about his body-shape
as he leans to dip the quill
brings their schooldays back, the voice
of old Matthew (learned and loving –
father, in the spirit, of his spirit)
telling by heart the visions of 'our'
Bard, 'the black, but brightest', while Tom's
hard-pressed nib is scratching
in his corner, such scatterings
of excited science! and himself,
'a wing with eyes', truant,
beyond the window, on the rippling hill.

Whatever he writes now will be,
he knows, both legacy and avowal.

12

*Written in November 1694 from Vaughan's last home, Holly Bush
Cottage, Scethrog, to John Aubrey, who had asked for information
about the Welsh Bards:*

[their vein of poetrie they] called *Awen* which in their language
signifies as much as Raptus, or a poetic furor; & (in truth) as
many of them as I have conversed with are (as I may say)
gifted or inspired with it. I was told by a very sober and know-
ing person (now dead) that in his time, there was a young lad
fatherless & motherless, & soe very poor that he was forced to
beg; butt att last was takn vp by a rich man, that kept a great
stock of sheep vpon the mountains not far from the place
where I now dwell, who cloathed him and sent him into the
mountains to keep his sheep. There in the summer time fol-
lowing the sheep & looking after their lambs, he fell into a
deep sleep; in wch he dreamt, that he saw a beautiful young
man with a garland of green leafs vpon his head, & a hawk
vpon his fist; with a quiver full of Arrows att his back, coming

towards him (whistling several measures or tunes all the way)
& att last lett the hawk fly att him, wch (he dreamt) gott into
his mouth and inward parts, & suddenly awaked in a great
fear & consternation: butt possessed with such a vein, or gift of
poetrie, that he left the sheep & went about the Countrey,
making songs vpon all occasions, and came to be the most
famous Bard in all the Countrey in his time.

13

> '. . . *this juggling fate*
> *Of soldiery.'*
> – 'Upon a cloak lent him by Mr J. Ridsley'

In a borrowed cloak, set
in stiff folds like an effigy.
Sparkling to marble in the frost.

Having no change of clothes
he slept (as he wrote) 'Adamite',
waking to find pale skin
pressed, overnight, by woven
coarseness into wrap-around text.

He seems to have pen and paper
to hand, even on the road.
His tone is jocular. He writes
a versified no-thanks note
to the lender, who also knows
what campaigning is.
                But now
O his mind flares as he tells
how his whiteness looks, that morning!
As if ancient camouflage
had come over him by magic,
making him Briton or Pict
part of the branchy snowscape,
camouflaged for battle in nothing
but hieroglyphics of imagination.

Catherine, his love (already his wife?),
could have read him blindfold. If only!

This he doesn't write. Twenty-four,
on the losing side, he keeps
the jokes coming. And yet,
his theme is a sense of self
as hermetic script, as a source
of holy or healing arts.

14

> *'Some syllables are swords.'*
> – 'Rules and Lessons'

The sickening sense
of being never again
what one once was.
Or worse, of having done
what nothing undoes.
In battle. Man to man.

Guts fresh from the cut,
the thrust of a blade –
his own, his writing, hand
in the guard of the sword?
Killing 'in the name of', but words,
all words, gone dead.

Sounds pass between people.
When words come back,
are they still words of the soul?
A survivor must seek
to rest the hilt of each syllable
on living rock.

Each poem a death
and a kind of regeneration.
With every breath,
failure, and liberation.

At the next breath
dread, anticipation.

Traumatised heart of stone!
You chose words crucified
in the Wars: those words alone
could heal through which peace died,
sectarian guilt, with your own,
transformed, purified.

15

For Adam and Liz.

'All things that be'
– 'The Bird'

As if by hand or whisper,
I have been woken to go
out, into that silence before the day.
The moon has withdrawn her whiteness. She sets,
now, on the ridge to the west,
a swollen russet globe,
and I remember
how in my lifetime we set foot on her
and found, under our feet, only loose clay.

Now, even wider, space opens
as the planet turns away.
The hillside with its iron-age fort blacks out
that lone disk. Only the stars,
now – those I see and those
teased into mind by astronomy –
mark the distance
back to the Beginning, forward to the End.
Still the breath in. Not yet the breath out.

Now neither moon nor sun. Dark
at its darkest. Before the dawn.
At its most silent. I feel the cold,
how naked my skin is under my coat.

146

Now, between night and light,
rehearsing the little I know of what is known,
I question my own work.
Language will end by destroying what I make.
At best, for a time, may hold what can't be told.

I look up and the stars too
are almost gone. The Plough
plunges blade first out of sight,
only its handle still bright and high.
Now with the naked eye
I can see the spin, how shadow
filters to blue
over green, and the sky, come nearer, begins to
mottle with blobs and rifts of dark and light.

All at once there's a twist of song,
piercing, passionate, a tall
fling of brilliance arcing into drops,
a woken life. Bright petals.
My brain, from this that falls
across it, stings at its own dull
self-hesitation,
my small heavy space lightening
suddenly, now, with a song self-care can't stop.

And the whole dark forest pours
with phrases my astonished ear
knows to be more than messages. The body
of each beast rejoicing in its transformation
from nothing to this. Dawn
happening at last, for ever,
now. The cause
not in question, not elsewhere. No pause
in whatever it is that is, hidden in and round me.

Then the birch, rising so still
on the light, a delicate flat
scatter of tiny leaves, shivers
and sways and lifts. My gazing mind
is shaken, with it, by that wind.

Pattern, colour – all that –
has begun to fill
the lit surface between hill and hill
while at my feet each grass-blade grows sharp, silvers.

Surely no inch untouched,
a made landscape. But matter.
With which we make, of which we are made.
Ancient and new, unpredictably changing.
It strikes through the robin's wing,
through the pruned rose, through the stare
of the dog, the thrust
of the weed, from a heap of domestic dust.
Day things. Among them, familiar, the human word.

Back in the house, every room
wakes and rings. My guests,
startled from sleep, remember how long
life really is. They sit in the kitchen
holding their steaming mugs, and one
who carries her first child tells
how it heard, in the womb!
With us already, it awaits the doom
of particular time and language, possibilities of song.

16

On the sudden death of a friend's wife.

'But life is, what none can express.'
– 'Quickness'

After the first shock, days
of (despite myself) thinking
'it could not have happened'
then raising my eyes and
being astonished instead that
the world was still there
and myself still seeing it.

148

In one of those first days
we saw her, the white doe,
slowly stepping between
the pine-dark edge
and a bright bulge of pasture
along our furthest fence.
One, two, three steps
only, as she passed,
moving only her long legs
behind the tiers of may-blossom.

By the time I got over there
to see if I could catch
sight of her still standing,
maybe, among the tree-trunks –
dark uprights of them floating
among bluebells, thickening
one behind the other until
no more spaces could be imagined
there wasn't a sign of her:
no tuft on the barbed wire
and the grass wasn't silver
where her hooves might have brushed it.

Was this the place? Or further
along the fence – perspectives
being what they are and we
too excited to count fence-posts?
And then against the light,
there were soft holes
in the grass, no more than that.
Her step had been so high,
so certain, as she passed.

I stood between the near scent
of the may and the vast wafting
dimness of so many bluebells.
My husband gone back in the house,
there was nothing to see but
the edge of an empty field and
a woman standing at the edge.

I found it hard to imagine
the weight of the doe, so flat
and white she looked, stepping
in profile behind the may,
her neck vertical as a periscope.
Any warmth she had breathed
into this air, invisible now,
must be drifting with the pale seeds
of the sallow in a great bank
of slow-moving forest breath.

In spite of myself, I strained
after a hint of hesitating white.
There was just a blueness there,
a rise and fall of distance
among closing trees. Dim
but, when focused on, intense.

17

> *'Nor are these births which we*
> *Thus suffering see*
> *Destroyed at all . . .'*
> – 'Resurrection and Immortality'

A few days ago
the footings had not been dug.
Grass grew undisturbed.

Now a lily lives
in a cube of still water
and a bud rises.

On the lily leaf,
two flies, smaller than rice grains.
Mexican stand-off?

Water bends its rim
down to the leaf's dry edges,
gleams without moving.

A wasp grips a reed,
leans to drink from her shadow
hanging in brightness.

While I write these words,
the bud must be rising,
too slow for my sight.

One fly flicks its wings.
The other flicks back. They leap.
It was fuck, not fight!

The wasp starts to throb,
pulling the wetness upward
with her two front legs.

The flies run apart,
across their lily-leaf and
straight onto water.

Far beneath them, weeds
breathe out a steady prickle,
air drawn from deep down.

Suddenly I see
what I am looking into –
blue sky filled with birds.

How lightly the flies
live between such distances,
on such a thinness!

On my page an ant
puzzles at the bitter trace
of ink not yet dry.

The lily's petals,
reaching a new dimension,
begin to open.

18

For Michael Srigley

'To search myself, where did I find
traces, and sounds of a strange kind . . .'
    – 'Vanity of Spirit'

Like me, you may have held
the weight of it, this gashed stone
made out of slow deposits
filtering down under pressure –
something I think your mind
would have held quite easily,
though your time could only guess
at the vastness of such transformations.

Whether a plough gauging
or mind-guided blade: newness
of human effort, like yours,
turning over, striking into,
balked always. And we're the same.

Centuries of spring water
seem to run under my fingers
as I trace the shallow Braille
of what might be bird or cross
or the strength of a horse on steel.

Your poems remember you
by the spring here, or on the ridge
with Llangorse Lake exhaling
its milky dreams or drawing
to itself an elixir of dew,
day slowly cooling.

A slanting light, the light
archaeologists love, reaches
the stone in your hands, a stone
you had never noticed, and now
highlighted hieroglyphics
flow from the stone over your hands.
It is as though the world

and you in it, hand-written
indecipherably with future histories,
emerge for a moment and now,
as you glimpse them, are already gone.

Doubtful light becomes day,
becomes night, and you
become a man holding a stone.
One who tries to believe
being dead could hold more meaning.

In the nature of mountain springs,
this one must have moved often,
and will move again but is,
as you heard that day, 'shrill':
a small clear fall
out of rock, still safe to cup
(returning the stone to its place)
in chilled fingers, and drink.

19

> *'A fatal sadness, such as still foregoes,*
> *Then runs along with public plagues and woes,*
> *Lies heavy on us . . .'*
> – 'Daphnis: An Elegiac Eclogue'

The tanks have halted on a dirt track
between two patches of ripening maize.
There are woods on a hillside behind
and a few thin calves are grazing loose
in a field without fences. The farms
have windows oddly dark: without glass.
There are no young men, save for soldiers,
and by now, we know what that must mean.

If it were you, I would have begged you
to take the gun and go. Then at least
we could both hope to meet again or
each might imagine the other safe.

All this is happening as I write words
and our Christian neighbour's maize rises
in a pale-headed unbroken chunk
not even bruised by last night's rain-storm.

The ground takes a lot of preparing
for maize. There will have been, there as here,
three layers at least of cow-muck, the rich
dark smell of it a real sign of spring.
The flags, with their tassels, are so tall
that last night you saw the fallow-deer vanish
among them, not even a ripple
to show where a shot might be put in.
Not that you would shoot them. Rabbits
are your targets (and no milky does).
Civilisation still hangs on here,
but I am not one of those who is
certain I'll never see my man crawl
to preserve life through a ripening crop.

O it's all those days – the ploughing
of winter grass into ribbed velvet,
the dips, the swellings and the mineral shades
coming to light, then the muck-spreader
back and back and back, the yearly jokes
(shouted across as the engine dies)
about the perfume of spring. It's the
shoulder-high shine. All that wasted work.

20

'. . . for marriage, of all states,
makes most unhappy, or most fortunates.'
– 'Isaac's Marriage'

We've beaten the lit water,
this man-made pool, to a phosphorescence,
a buffeting mesh of slender
light-loops, opening, closing,
twisting across each other,
taut edges riding up
into our own mouths and eyes, a pat,
a whisper, a sizzle at the ear.
Here, every movement we make
echoes through water so that the soft
weight of it, wind on the skin,
carries our strokes like voices.
The whole body hears them.

Your water-voice reaches me
and mine you among messages
sent by the bodies of strangers.
If now and then we touch – really,
flesh to flesh – it's like becoming
aware again of a separation.
The pool is a huge bed,
such a flow of transparent sheets!
And these others we swim with
(their cool edges, their brightnesses)
might be lovers not quite forgotten.

I look up into wooden rafters,
a tree of tangled reflections –
some youthful memory of lying
by a river, between root and branch.
The space between must be filled
with aerial impulses of light
silently clashing above our heads.
And over there, behind you,
on the sill of the gym-room window,
the back of a head bobs,

jogging tirelessly into the telly's
smaller, brighter square.
Boxes within boxes. Pain leaking,
like joy, from one to the other.

21

'And in thy shades, as now, as then
We'll kiss, and smile, and walk again.'
– 'Upon the Priory Grove, His Usual Retirement'

Flutter of clouded gold. A last
sip of nectar, at the Grove's edge,
in a mild warm smell of thistles.
I think of the long heart afloat
in white blood, the signals it sends.
A kind of prophecy. Like his
inadmissible forebodings.
How else will this creature decide
to venture from local breezes
up into the huge airflow south?
So that where it has always lived
becomes: contours of air-pressure,
untouched, untastable distance.

Some such instinct shapes what he writes,
the way butterflies smell the soft
underfoot purple, open out
with resting body, though trembling
in the sunshine from wing to wing.
Something he did foresee. But not
what, not when. Such a clutter of
sad wings, poison ivy, old age,
innocence about to be lost!
That's not it. Already migrant,
he knows that 'now' should become 'then' –
through words at least – before it's gone.

'These leaves', he wrote, 'this air'. Catherine
soon to be presence too: 'as now',
he wrote, sure of her kiss, her smile.

Leaf shapes, in-between-leaf spaces,
tremble and shift across his page
as across this one, so the words
are obscured, picked out, on the move.
Where he wrote, I read – handwriting
just print now. But I still feel it,
amazing terror of new love.

'As now, so then', he wrote, his 'then'
some future: an invocation.
But for me, 'then' is their two cries
joined a moment: 'our laid echo'.

I watch the bounce of the thistle,
wings turning dark against the sky.
Survival. To do with distance?

22

Remembering my mother.

'Settle my house, and shut out all distractions
        That may unknit
My heart . . .'
                    – 'The Match'

My thumb pulls the blade through,
sounding like steps in snow.
I notice this, having looked
away over white fields –
but not snow yet, just dew.
What was a round thing
uncurls airily, bounces
(as I peel) towards the littered
sheen of water.
                    The back
of my head suggests to me panes
flowered with frost at daybreak.
I sense long-ago neatness,
six-year-old body in hand-knitted
woollies. There is a stairwell,

I think, somewhere quite close.
An orderly house pivots
round someone else's work.

                    Now that
I do the work, it's different:
no child will imagine me
the centre of her world.

                Her cheeks
were flushed as mine are, her hands
were scarred by some strange clumsiness
with hot ovens and knives.

My hands begin to ache.
The one which turns each apple
between finger-tips and thumb-heel.
The one which strokes off the spiral.
Snow, yes. A cold globe,
diffusing its fleshy light.

Again, a sudden sense:
the creak of a thickening snowball
between cupped palms, the browning
of cut snow each side of a door.

I'm less remembering than remembered.
Years, since I did this. Years
more since I watched her do it.
My hands are not only my mother's
but my own younger ones. The past
is my body now, like layers
of a poem discovering itself.

Starting each fruit, I look forward
to its tough chalice – a delicate
lantern, and those dark flames
my task will have to waste.
Now the big pan is heaped
with half-moons, thin, sugared
over the top – sweet sparkle
to be picked off in slices, till a hot
white froth puffs to engulf them.

158

What about jelly next time?
Crab-apples, wild and hard,
with cracked skins. I imagine
how the lichen will fall on my face
as I knock them with tight-shut eyes.
Each action has history. My thumb,
I know, will be scuffed by the knife
and stained, as I halve and throw
the whole fruit in – I like
to feel, for many days,
the damage of something completed.

While slowly the puree is cooling,
I let them emerge – mornings
when, too early for her liking,
I crept down to witness alchemy.
The fire would be barely lit.
A little smoke, and a crackle
of warmth in bright cold air.
The chair would be still upturned.
I would tip up the glass bowl
beneath the bulbous dangle
of doubled muslin, be told off
as I made it sway, still dripping,
over misty viscous pink.
Not much, but the real thing.
Then the warmed sugar, stirred
with a white-wood spoon she kept
unstained all year just for this.
Then the mist in the pan changed
to a thin grey spume splitting
(as she skimmed) over ruddy gold.

My job now to open the window,
hold out a clear thin slick
to the fields' breath and then,
against the light, slide in
the nail of my little finger
and peer for the rise of wrinkles.
Then eat the skimmings as she filled.

Flames in a chilly room still
make me catch my breath. Or grass
as if moonlit on winter mornings.
Soon, I'll have hot jars cooling
and be glad such clarity comes
of whole apples, pips and all.
I can hear the satisfied tap
of her nail on the concave shine.
Tight tops, fit for storage.

23

Thinking of Denize Morgan carrying the Vaughan twins.

And make hills blossom like the vales . . .
Till from them, like a laden bee,
I may fly home, and hive with thee.
– 'The Bee'

Her heart-beat flows round them, in them, like a footfall.
Not yet time to breathe. There are no choices.
There is no guilt. The world is making them.

On the sill of her window, by a guttering candle,
the Book's left open. On its linen pages,
thoughts in English, which they'll learn to read by.

Already translated, twice over. In the starlight,
a cock's lizard eye suddenly blazes.
His blood is warm now, but still remembers.

Likewise, twin foetuses are shape-changers.
Two becoming one. One becoming two again.
Amoeba. Fish-curl. Mammalian limb-buds.

The cock's cry pulses out into the darkness,
calls up the bouncing brilliance of daybreak.
Westward, tree-tops shimmer in the window.

She turns, stretches. Where she left it, *Genesis*
heaps open against the dawn. She thinks of Tyndale.
No-one can choose their time. What changes!

Orphaned, widowed, remarried by twenty,
at least she has round her the things of childhood –
the walls of Newton, the sounds of her farm yard.

When her parents were living, I guess she scrambled
from this very house (in the years of Elizabeth)
to pick, on the Allt, little bunches of flowers.

She'd still see the magic in the clear bright honey
her bees make of them. Would love to gather
herself, from the hive – the brittle lattice.

I lend her my memories: the cool sweetness,
the crumbled chewy cells, and that ancient
right, and sin – humankind's plunder.

Who else would have passed to their linked spirits
such a sense of matter? Its crumbling and containing?
Or voiced, from print-strokes, a beat of life-blood?

'Nec erubuit silvas habitare Thalia':
two boys in Wales receiving that message,
time and space between. Elegant. Primitive.

'Honey in woods'. Wild bees of inspiration.
Maybe they tracked them, found out the roof-nook
in old St Bridget's, where the bees nested?

Sixteen seventy-six, its bell was founded.
For a 'bee-hive' bell-tower of 'no known architecture'.
(Image from childhood. Image in a poem.)

On a model suggested by the local doctor?
Or to honour him? Or by grateful readers,
recalling the dark years, a shut up building?

It's gone, the church where their mother worshipped,
where Thomas was rector. Henry's traces lie now
in the shade of a new, inaccessible spire.

These days, in the valley, the steady bell,
when it steps our way, brings few of us back.
Some literalists. Some hearers of metaphor.

161

By his tomb, eyes closed, I listen to its beat.
Brood on how births bring change. How a life
may transform other lives by the choices it makes.

There's the road you took on your war-horse, and later
on your doctor's nag. And here you worshipped,
in a space whose walls were bowed by the bell-tower.

I open my eyes on a wild-flower knot,
made of common species, with a twisted stalk
to hold them together, laid on your tomb.

What a walker might damage. Someone who reads
both you and nature. And would honour both.
A bee is giving its blessing, they're so fresh!

CODA

Magnolia

I have watched for weeks, just how dawn flings down a hint
of shade from the top of the hill, a sway and flicker
of distant pine, then foxglove, elder, blackthorn
at a widening angle. I note where it lies the longest,
so that morning dew won't singe them, the fleshy pale
extravagant blooms. Let them dream the touch
of pterodactyls, all the tropical vanished things,
and wake to a nuzzle of bees, a core vibrating.

Each spring, for years, when I caught their upward showers
seeming to defy gravity, I would feel my feet
hold me suddenly upside down to the weight of the earth.
It wouldn't take much, it seemed, to release me, down
through that deep blue curve to the weightless dark. But
    magnolia
rhymes with suburbia! Always, a something missing
from my sense of them (as if we had made them ourselves
to be glorious for us) would stop me bringing one home.

How wrong can you get? First ever of flowering plants,
survivor of dinosaurs – as Takhtajan said,
without their kind, our own kind couldn't appear.
I knock from its plastic tub my few pounds'-worth
of Cretaceous forest rim. While my fingers loosen
the tangled root-ball, ease it into leafy soil,
a message must begin to flow. I guess how the life
takes hold, both ways, unhurried in-between my hands.

Stag Beetle

I almost put my hand on him,
big, black, fearsome and
as beautiful as an illustration.
Bending closer to look,
I fancied I could smell the gloss
of old paper, see a ghost of Latin
in the scribble of the rendering's pock-marks.

He was tight in there, like a fly
dried to a net curtain –
hard to pick off in one piece.
But I couldn't leave him, dog-height
by the front door, at the mercy
of a bucket-rim or the hip
of a running child.
                    I cursed
myself too for the blue-green pellets
in the garden wall. Might he feed
on them, or on slugs?
                    Such quiet
could be cunning, could be sickness. I took in
how little my bones would show
if I were concealed inside them.

The next bit must have been amazing,
wafted upright through the air,
rising and falling to a drum-beat,
nothing to explain it but two
warm patches at either edge.
His legs, with slow dignity,
bent at their hinges to seek
a firmer accustomed darkness.
Even the great jaws opened
just a little, suggesting he was doubtful.

But he froze when his feet touched ground
in a safer spot. And it wasn't
till his angel, his bad, his good,
his uncertain angel, had left him,

thundering away with its shadow
across concrete, that he must have gripped
the earth underfoot and rolled off on it
too fast to be seen again.

Butterflies

For Geoff Palmer

What I remember is the flash,
blue opening out all round me,
and for a second the impetus of reading
kept my eyes on the page so the back
of my head was filled with flicker,
something like a perfume of colour,
something like a turning wave
full of sun and sparkle and glitter
and the lovely whoosh of it hanging
about to break, seemingly for ever.

When I pass the spot, I see it
somewhere, not quite so brilliant,
never so startling. In the mind.
Only in the mind. And although
the ground has flattened again
and is jewelled with moss, and sedge
and rush recolonise from the rim,
at the heart of this patch of land
there are still the hidden gashes
of tyre-marks, of dragged logs,
a season of useful work.

Since you are with me again
I tell you again, and you listen.
For a moment we can barely hear
each other's thoughts, a helicopter
slanting down to see us here
then veering off, searching, searching.
A body was found in the woods
while we talked of death. And I thought
of sitting on this changed ground
before the change, how my presence
wore away into the sough and buzz
of bees and trees and the brush
of wings coming apart in sunshine.

Smoke

We roll back the dirty straw, like lino,
folded in cracked sheets, and wheel it
to where, when it's damp with drizzle, we'll set
a match to it, and to this year's dead.

Our ewes, heavy, puffing a little, graze
in the rain. Lambs that will burn are still
learning to live in that moving ocean.
Nothing to do, in our own time, but wait.

Drifting to sleep in bed, I wrap
my hand round your heavy, dreaming fist.
My fingers are soft, my nails trimmed
for internal work, almost to the quick.

Early, my torch-beam travels. Quiet heaps
of breathing ewes. In the corner, there's one
akimbo, with teats tucked forward. A lamb
is butting her, its twin just a hard cold sliver.

In my dream, we were creatures whose blood flowed
from somewhere else. We floated like astronauts,
with umbilical cords that showed how weak
we remain, how little we make life happen.

Survivors gang up, rush round. When the wind's
gone down, we'll set the tall smoke going.
It'll drift through the spangled willow. By then
those tips will be yellow with pollen. Forgetful.

If we remember ourselves after death,
I hope we may seem as light and bright
as that scarcely-contaminated air, twisting
higher and higher. Drawn to new weather.

Guilt

Back-lit, their folds edge to edge,
new rose-leaves wag and glow
in the first light wind of morning.
The shade of a small thing flies
from left to right on a ripple
of net, that's all, but I know
it's the robin again, whose mate
in her ziggurat of moss, at the rose's
tangled stem, broods tight
on five pale pebbles.
Her breast-bone, its warm skin,
will be bared to curves that only
my eye has touched – their cluster
a fresh-laid shine.

How my fingers
stiffened with guilt when I got
to the hidden nest, in their grip
a tuft of grass, snail-damp.
That meticulous tower, that hand's breadth
of tapering roundness. That cup
at its tip, deep-spun to bird size.
And across what should have been sway
of dapple, a hard-edged shadow.
And in it, what surprising brightness!

At the same time next day, I looked.
With luck, she was not scared off,
just away somewhere feeding. At once,
before she might catch me, I cut
long sprays of holly, stuck them in
where the grass had stood, a barrier
to wind and sun. Protection.

Each day, when I look, she has laid
one more – till at last an eye
meets mine, so direct that I blink.

Now I watch at a distance while her mate
brings worms, or the two of them chatter
by the pool, or not a thing happens.

At hatching, the holly should still
be sharp if not green, should put off
that feral cat whose paw-marks
ring-a-rosy my car, whose cry
every night is hawk-like, whose body,
save in dreams, I know I'll not see.

Yellow Meadow-Ants in Hallowed Ground

For Colin Titcombe, naturalist and teacher

I need to displace myself. I need to see,
when the tip of my finger disturbs the alignment of dust
over their open holes, how a human hand
might seem (as to them) nothing more than the foot of a vole.

I need to feel, more than I need to see,
as if I had helped to make it, that airy mass
hung in the solid dark of a marked-out grave.
An ancient pasture healing the shock of death.

I need to be glad, I must be, such intricate bronze,
such tiny aggressive life, can thrive as if cut
of spade, as if cry, were no more than the passing tricks
of storm or flood, or of geological heave.

Spare, like sea-shore stuff, dry grasses stand
deep in these ants' displacement of inner ground.
When the tips catch wind, my veins seem wrapped round the
        quiver
of those hidden columns, as if I had left myself.

Cave Trout

I can hardly remember them. Clearer
those dark striations into darkness,
the limestone layering, and your torch
a distorted sun slipping down
from stone to pits of air
to a shine-line of water.
                              But did
I see them, where surface glitter
gave way to see-through? A movement
as if water displaced water,
something like an eye-socket ridging
that floating translucence? A muteness
of memory – like censorship that closes,
too often, a dream, as one wakes
and turns the mind round to see it –
clicks off the vision.
                              Remember
how you clicked the torch off? And we knew
for breathtaking seconds what they,
their sighted ancestors, knew
just after the river first broke,
then for centuries. And then, the slow
change. How flesh was withdrawing
its denser flakes, pink spots,
becoming as dark, or as light, as water.
How whatever had met the sun,
by making eyes, had nothing
any more to respond to. But still
the huddle of spawn must bring back,
from time to time, a body
more fitted to pebble-flecked shallows,
an eye desirous of messages.

What would such creatures make
of their strange selves? Of darkness
perceived? Of scales pigmented
by inklings of reflected light?

Already, at the cave mouth,
we saw mountains as blur, had to blink
to restore their shapes, our horizons.

When I call them to mind, the short
dry grass, the slant of paths
eroding to rock, my desire
insists on sea-floor, on rock-fall
deep into water: on surfaces
open to the sky. Catastrophes
that may not destroy but liberate.

A Matter of Scale

It's a matter of scale at first. We park up
for a fungus foray. But instead, it's the forest,
the whole of it, that catches the gaze of our group
so that we stand, dizzied, like people
hanging out washing, with heads bent back
looking to the tops where the leaves are drifting
north to south – but so slowly, slowly,
air seems like water. Huddled down here
we're too small to feel wind and the trees
are small in that draining depth. We say,
well, nothing significant, but enough to share
a sense of surprise. It's eyes down, then,
for the beech-litter-orange *Boletus* or a frill
of white *Crepidotus* on a fallen twig,
Grifola's fountain of flesh or the pink
of *Mycena Pura*, alabaster glow
of *Oudemansiella* on a blackening branch.
Or this, or this. Most of all, the magic
of magnification, millimetres exploding
into shape and shine and translucence beyond
the coarseness of our fingers.
                              Today we have with us
a woman profoundly deaf. On her voice
the shapes of speech, the words, are roughened,
and sometimes she gestures on an open palm.
Illiterate, I watch and guess, and reply
with gestures I have to make up, translating
myself, till she guesses.
                              And the feel of that
stays with me, now, as I raise my eyes
to the mirage behind the trees, Australian
masses, rosy Devonian – a delta,
buckled till the crest snapped open
to an empty dazzle. The valleys below
lie quiet, hardworked to domestic surface.
Whatever is gone seems a bridging gesture
of utter silence.
                              Her hands reach out.
I can't resist, either – the touch on my palm

the top of one floor and, rough on the back,
the base of another, and the space between
where my arm slides in. Fossils of a kind.
Of ghostly varying waters. Turbulence
of tumbled, fist-sized quartz, rounded
before it was dropped, pressed down to this spot,
this very spot, so I'd hate to dislodge it.
Some other layers hold a pin-head glitter,
tracing a weaker outflow, the colours,
cross-cut, of distant or of softer sources.
Then stagnant washes, sand-fine, worn out
to these airy seams.
                    Backing off, I see life,
up there, of a kind we don't use the word for.

Later, I'm looking at spores on my palm
under magnification. They look like sand
on those ridges of shining flesh, a scatter
of silica clinging there too, the distinction
so much less obvious than it used to be.